21st CENTURY SALES MANAGEMENT

21st CENTURY SALES MANAGEMENT

Peter Chambers

To my wife, Suzanne.

First published in 2004 by Management Books 2000 Ltd
Forge House, Limes Road
Kemble, Cirencester
Gloucestershire, GL7 6AD, UK
Tel: 0044 (0) 1285 771441/2
Fax: 0044 (0) 1285 771055
E-mail: mb.2000@virgin.net
Web: www.mb2000.com

Printed and bound in Great Britain by Biddles of King's Lynn

British Library Cataloguing in Publication Data is available

ISBN 1-85252-451-0

Contents

1

Getting to Grips with Sales Management

So, why did you buy this book? It is most likely that, for a variety of reasons, you need to step back and take a fresh look at the way the sales function works in your company. Whether you own the company or have just joined it, the best way to start is at the top and that means management. Sales is no different from any other part of a business in that you will not get a high performance department without high performance management. But, what is sales management? Is it all smoke and mirrors, bribery and bullying? It is none of those things. Sales management is a skilled, logical and intelligent role that demands the disciplines and planning of any other senior position. The purpose of this book is to show how good management through order and structure can support the development and success of sales people. Successful staff make a successful business.

In terms of selling, where are you starting from? Do you own a growing business and managing sales is a burden or even a distraction? Perhaps you want to recruit a sales manager and need to know the elements of the job. Were you a sales person but yesterday your boss promoted you to sales manager? At first, you were full of proud excitement; but now? No longer one of the lads, you are expected to drive, motivate and get results. What if you are an ambitious sales person and keen to get on the management ladder? Who will guide and mentor you? What skills do you need to develop?

Perhaps the most difficult to define situation is if you are the CEO or Managing Director of a large organisation. You know that the sales function functions but instinctively feel that all is not right. Of all the key departments, sales is the one that seems most opaque in methodology. The output as orders is obvious but how it gets them is more nebulous. It also costs the most considering the number of people involved. Is it a high performance department or just muddling along, afraid to change because 'it has always been done that way'.

When you get a management consultancy or bright MBA to look at it, you get lots of standard management theory or marketing but a suspiciously shallow investigation of the actual selling. In a sense you want to get under the skin of the department but do not know how.

Let us be clear about what this book does set out to do and what it cannot do.

This book aims to:

- position the sales department or function in terms of what it will deliver to the business – this will help short term and long term planning
- differentiate between sales and marketing, close cousins but very different
- identify the personal characteristics of the best sales people and how to recruit them
- understand the business in sales terms and structure the team to deliver now and in the future
- examine the basics of how to manage and control the team
- identify day to day issues and how to deal with them
- highlight the difficult area of pay and commissions
- consider other ways to sell.

What it does not offer to do includes:

- using management to turn bad sales people into good sales people – some people, for a variety of reasons, try to do jobs that are not suitable for them

- tell you that the job of sales manager is easy and all you need is a few processes and check sheets – the job is complex, challenging and will always stretch your abilities.

Sales management blends intellectual and personal skills to a degree uncommon in many other business functions. There is a whole chapter on the nature of sales people. To be a successful sales manager you will need many of those characteristics. Be analytical with yourself as you read it and be honest about how you shape up. Then, consider that your success depends on identifying and encouraging those characteristics in others.

There is one last point to be made in this chapter and it is a vital one. Honesty and integrity are not normally mentioned in the same breath as sales and marketing. But, of all the functions, sales needs them most. Lack of honesty and integrity will corrode not just internal relationships but also relationships with your customers.

**Integrity starts at the top, therefore with you.
Never forget that.**

2

Image and Role – Sales as Part of the Organisation

You are probably keen to get to the nuts and bolts of sales management later in the book. The chapter on the characteristics of sales people will be well scrutinised. You are likely to have made an early visit to commissions and bonuses, as money must be at the heart of motivating sales people. Even if you do not read this chapter first be sure to read it soon. It deals with matters not normally discussed in business. The first part tackles the image of selling. Let's be honest, selling is not in the same social league as brain surgery. Time then to address the issue and work on it. The second part deals with how the sales function fits into the rest of the organisation. On the surface it may seem obvious. It is not quite as simple as it sounds, so some thought on it now can save much aggravation later.

Image

Sales does have an image problem. If you are not from a sales background, the issue of image may cloud your judgement. Judgement concerning the type of people you want to employ and how you manage them.

Sales is associated with spin, wild promises or, even actual lies. Stories of mis-selling – particularly financial services – have led to widely publicised compensation. The demands of the job are seen to require a tolerance of various depravities. The common view is, to sell a product or a service, some economy of the truth was required. Hence, a salesman was someone inherently untrustworthy. Good fun, mind you, smooth talking and always ready to buy a drink, paid from an inexhaustible expense account. Literature, plays and films are full of the stereotype. Freed from the ever watchful eye of the manager at the factory, the salesman roamed from doubtful sale to romantic conquest until just retribution was exacted. The problem is seen to be one of selling and the sales person rather than being a management issue or the culture of management in the organisation.

This image is reinforced by a lack of knowledge of the sales process. Selling is not taught as a serious academic subject. Marketing, the close companion of sales, lends itself better to the structure of being taught with facts, statistics and well known case studies. Many job advertisements ask for a marketing qualification, confident that they exist and, like other qualifications, give some base line of credibility to the candidate. While marketing can be studied at first degree level, selling is not and is rarely found as a core element of business degrees. It is relegated to being a vocational subject and is done rather than being studied. Training courses abound promising to turn your flabby sales team into well honed selling machines. These courses produce certificates grandly signed by the organiser but even the better known ones cannot guarantee that the participants were not asleep most of the time. In fact, there is little reason why selling cannot be built into an academic course considering some of the vocations that can be laughably studied at degree level.

So, sales has languished in the shadow world of skills defined by personality. Experience is thought to be the key, backed up by a nimble persuasiveness and various black arts. It often involves much entertaining of clients, because *who* you know is crucial. There are also people who 'owe a favour' and can help make the impossible happen. Out of this alchemy comes a stream of orders, or at least reasons for the imminent arrival of orders. The continuance of orders requires golfing skills, lunches and overnight stays in hotels.

For the entrepreneur or small-business person needing to expand the business, the issue of sales and salespeople becomes a looming problem. Very frequently, the business owner or manager is not from a sales background. Often, the owner is technical or production oriented and the business started through an interest in a technology, hobby or sport. Sometimes a business is bought because it seems a sound opportunity. By diligent management and careful finances, it should prosper. In these circumstances, there is a belief that, given good design, efficient manufacture and an accurate description of the product, then a steady stream of orders will result. The same is true of service industries from cleaning contracts to warehousing.

However, it is found that the orders are not as strong as hoped. Rivals with inferior products or services grab the business. This is frustrating and it is easy to conclude that the competition exaggerate their abilities or even lie. Worse, they may even be thought to make disparaging or false claims about your own company to win the order. When a call is made to the lost customer to ascertain why a company with an inferior product has won, the reasons are clearly ridiculous. It is easy for the struggling business owner to believe that he or she is the victim of sharp practice. The other company must have a sales force that cheat.

The idea that his own sales team, if he has one, has merely been out-sold is difficult to grasp. Buyers always buy the better product, right? Wrong. There are ample case studies to show that having the best product gives no insurance or certainty of success. The failure of Sony's Betamax standard is perhaps the best example of a technically superior product losing out to a poor competitor. That was a marketing failure rather than sales but the same principles apply.

The business owner has to face the issue of strengthening the sales team. In many SMEs, there may not even be a distinct sales function. Inquiries would be dealt with an ad hoc team of technical staff and administrators. Sales may have been delegated to someone who is more comfortable with customers, perhaps an older employee who can remember previous products and has empathy with enthusiasts among the customers. Often the senior manager or business owner does the majority of sales. While disparaging sales as a function, the importance is sub-consciously recognised in that the owner likes to represent the business to the customer. When this is obviously inadequate, allowing others to do the selling means grasping the problem. Too often it just means grasping the image.

Creating a sales team and then dealing with and motivating salespeople are skills of which many managers and business owners have no experience. There are two significant differences between salespeople and most other employees.

The first is that they cannot be chosen by the normal selection criteria. As mentioned above, there are few, if any, formal qualifications in selling. Selling is a difficult and complex job. To get a person with the required intellectual capital suggests that a degree is very desirable. A degree in what subject? As we will read later, strong intellectual capital is necessary but a degree in a subject with no relation to selling is a poor guide. There are sales training courses offered by private companies but they tend to be short and offer no assurance of quality or that the student has benefited. Salespeople move into selling from other disciplines. The reasons for moving are varied but it is unlikely that they went through a rigorous training schedule as they made the transition. Marketing is different and it is possible to find staff with relevant qualifications. The copious supply of data makes marketing more obviously analytical so easier to make into an academic subject. However, marketing is not selling and to see why, read the next chapter. The skills are different and moving from one to the other is no more straightforward then any other career change. On the CV of a sales person, the qualifications are interesting but the experience and track record is vital.

The second key difference is that, once employed, the salesperson is out of sight much of the time. Managerial scrutiny is more difficult. Is the salesperson in front of a customer or sitting at home? This is uncomfortable enough with field sales people operating from your office, but, what of a remote salesperson, operating from home in another part of the country? This issue is a source of considerable tension between management and sales staff. When times are tough and orders are vital, the integrity of the sales people is paramount.

If these were not serious enough problems on their own they are made worse by the fact that, in general, sales people are expensive to keep. Apart from the salaries, they need to be kept on the road; cars, meals, hotels and so on push up the costs of employment. As a minimum, to keep a sales person on the road will cost 50% of base salary. Commissions and bonuses are another tricky area which can drain money for little benefit if not planned carefully.

Once the sales person is hired, properly and expensively equipped, and knows what to sell, the image of your company rests on the performance of that person. For many customers, their only contact with your company is via the sales person. Not only the commercial success of the business is in their hands but also they can tie you into legal commitments or obligations. And this is even before we get to mis-selling. Stories in the press on aggressive or illegal selling can tarnish the reputation of a company from which recovery may be difficult. Having to dismiss staff is often traumatic; the investment you need to put into a sales person makes this step even more destructive.

Here then is the dilemma. The sales function can be the main way your business represents its image to the customer. It should convey quality, reliability, honesty, integrity, innovation or any other significant advantage of your company. The sales person should have the intelligence to add value to the customer decision, navigate objections and solve problems. However, the sales profession has no academic qualification to the equivalent of accountancy or engineering. The image may deter the best qualified to take up selling. The elements of sales staff selection and management are rarely taught adequately.

Why labour all of the above? Because, until the wrong or negative image of the profession is understood and firmly binned, it is not possible to plan a professional team. This book cannot solve all the issues but it can tackle how to recruit the right type of people and manage them effectively. With good management and selection, the well run sales team can turn a mediocre business into a thriving success story. You can control the business, collect data on opportunities, monitor the competition and help develop products to match the market. The important step is to stop regarding sales as a black art controlled by stick and carrot and see it as a well planned and executed core part of the business.

Making sales fit

The role of sales within the organisation may seem obvious; to get orders. This hides a wealth of issues which, if not addressed, can lead to tensions and loss of performance.

The role of sales goes to the core of the company. Take two extremes; first a coal mine. Critical is the cost and volume of extraction. Profitability is mainly getting the optimum rate for these two criteria. The role of sales is to sell the resulting output. Selling more may be totally wrong as production may not be capable of increase. Selling less will result in stockpile. The sales function is not the driver of the company fortunes. It is important but subservient to production. Secondly, at the other extreme, in a reseller business, the product mix and stocking volumes depend on the performance of the sales function. With this type of company, marketing may be as important as sales and especially for the consumer market, may be totally marketing led.

Most businesses are more complex to define in this way. A company in high technology may appear to be a simple batch manufacturing operation. However, who really controls the output and product mix may be more subtle to determine. The issue for the business owner is political rather than simple management. Once the sales function is improved it can highlight internal power struggles over who calls the shots. In the high technology company, the engineers and technologists may well feel that they are the core of the company and define the nature of the products and how they should be marketed and sold. Here, employing sales people or managers who want to dictate features of a product in order to meet what they feel are market needs will lead to internal stresses and strains.

Hence, you need to be quite clear on the role of sales so that the business is improved and not a departure lounge for hacked off executives. Not only may key people leave but also you may recruit the wrong replacements to compound the problem. One way to start is to go through a simple checklist to broadly define your company.

1 Sales led

Broadly, not a lot happens until you get an order. An example is the reseller mentioned earlier. Whether it is feet on the street selling or telesales, success will be closing orders. You stock what sells and abandon what does not. Critical is cost of sale, buying price and margin. Often the buying price is fixed with a set range of discounts from the manufacturer. EU competition laws have removed much of the favourable treatment certain resellers could obtain to beat their competitors. Now the sales force must articulate value by service or add extra and unique value to enhance the sale.

Build-to-order manufacturing may be sales led but there is a trap. If the core competence is a particular technology or design, the owner must balance the sales function very delicately with the other individuals or departments. It is possible to have a core competence in a design but with an aggressive sales led company culture. It's how you do it that counts.

2 Marketing led

Your company may have a sales team but, if your product can be bought by someone without speaking to a salesperson, your company is definitely marketing led. This is especially true if someone with little product knowledge does the selling. The best example is something sold in a shop. Brand image, features, benefits and presentation are key to success. Cars are an interesting combination of marketing and sales strategies. The manufacturer spending money on marketing the image while the showrooms employ salespeople to close the deal.

3 Production led

If the business is driven by the limitations or advantages of the production process, typically continuous manufacturing, then sales is constrained by what the factory can do. Sub-contract work also fits into this, selling the capacity to manufacture.

4 Technology led

Many of the IT companies were started by engineers who not only satisfied existing markets with good products but created completely new markets. A heavy investment in research and development meant a constant stream of new products, each one more capable and, usually, more complex then before. The job of sales and marketing was to find customers. While the sales teams could act as a channel for customer comments and criticisms, the forward strength of the company was firmly in the grip of the technologists. Only they knew what was possible with much of their thinking shrouded in secrecy. Surprisingly, this type of company is the preserve of the well-honed sales teams. With no agonising over product details and having little control over what they sell, all effort goes into pure selling.

How much do you need to worry about the role of sales? If you own the business or are the CEO, you should have sales and marketing represented at the most senior level. At this level the aims and objectives of the company should be known and understood. The key drivers of the business are agreed, with the contribution and boundaries of each function clearly articulated. Is this an accurate description of your business? If you give less than a resounding yes then you need to worry. Which function drives the business is a constant source of aggravation. This book cannot help with your other functions but knowing how to position selling will give you the chance to make it as effective as possible within your business. If you are the sales manager, particularly a new sales manager, knowing how you fit in can make the difference between a good useful career and an eventual departure to a more hospitable environment.

3

First, Manage Yourself

Let us assume that you have just been recruited to be sales manager of National Widgets Ltd. You were a rank and file sales person before and this is your big break for management. The following rules also apply if you are the business owner looking after sales. If you are the owner and have recruited a sales manager you might want to use this chapter to clearly communicate what you are expecting.

In a later chapter, the characteristics of the best sales people are identified. Here we will do the same for sales managers. In popular opinion, how do the best sales managers get results? Of course it is a mixture of stick, carrot and bullying. And the key characteristics of the manager? To be able to drive, pressure, ramrod or squeeze performance out of the team. Is any other part of a well managed company managed like that? Not a chance and there would be big trouble if it was. So, assuming you do not want blood on the walls, here is what you need to do well so that you end up with a high performance sales team.

There is a short list of key skills and actions you need to do well to be successful. They may well cover 80% of everything you need and you can get the other 20% from the vast number of management books. These are:

- recruitment
- strategy
- setting goals and boundaries
- engaging with the team.

It is a short list that conceals much effort and the exercise of intellect. It does not include selling – that was your old job. Having said that, see how you match up with the best sales people in chapter 5. It is assumed that if you were successful at sales you should score well. If you are not from a successful sales background, then add those sales characteristics to this chapter. Not happy with that? Read it anyway, recruit in those skills and keep this book in your top drawer. We will look at the key things you need to do well in turn.

Recruitment

This is the most important and fundamental part of your job. Get this right and all the rest is possible. Get it wrong and you will constantly struggle and firefight. There is a chapter on recruitment that gives the basics. Read it with the preceding chapter on the characteristics of sales people. If you inherit a team, then meet them as soon as possible as individuals. Treat the meeting as if it was a job interview. Take notes because later you may have to restructure the team to enable your strategy and better serve the company.

If you have a team in place with the right skills and attitude, management becomes an exciting pleasure. You can get to grips with honing the team into an effective selling force. They will feel the buzz and want to do better. Training becomes part of development and will allow you to fine tune the individuals to make best use of their skills.

If you get a mixed bag, then hard luck – the job is never too easy. Take time to assess the team and discuss with your boss or other senior management. There are a variety of reasons why sales people may not be doing the job well. It could be staleness or lack of focus. If you have been recruited due to the poor performance of your predecessor, then watch out for de-motivation. Don't forget, one of the team may have wanted your job and got turned down. You will soon find out who it was. With others, sales may have seemed a promotion but now they are struggling. Quite often, the company and products have moved on but some sales people cannot move as well. Your ability to be analytical and sensitive at the same time will be stretched. It is tempting to be tough as you are the new boy on the block. It shows you can hack the job. However, if there are tough decisions to be made, you might want to work out the strategy first so as to be seen to be in control. You have to be clever to succeed in being tough.

While good recruitment will define the nature of your success, you cannot do it until you have a strategy. Therefore, if you need to hire, put it on the back burner for now and think about strategy.

Strategy

It is no use having a good team if you cannot put them to good use. You may have wondered why the second chapter of the book had a section on the place of sales within the organisation. Strategy is not just about getting orders. It is about getting the orders that the business needs to prosper. The strategy changes as the company changes but, at any point in time, you need to be clear on the strategy and communicate it well to the team.

The strategy will define what orders the business needs and how you will get them. For example, a key part of the strategy could call for a lower cost of sale. To do this, your sales team could be radically different in the future. Fewer end user field sales, more telesales and internet marketing. Or the opposite – a concentration on fewer high-margin complex sales with skilled field sales people.

You must get this part right or it will cause any number of senior management problems. You can design and formalise the sales strategy but it must be owned jointly with the top team. If it is not fully accepted, the sales team will see their work undermined. If the sales team do not know or understand the strategy, they can never be fully effective. Both you and the team have to be able to deal with the normal company tensions.

The chapter on getting organised goes through the mechanics of putting the strategy into action. Before you can define the strategy you need to do plenty of homework. Once you have a sensible plan, ensure that everyone buys into it.

Setting goals and boundaries

So far your analytical skills and those of assessment have been well exercised. Now is the time to test your judgement. You have defined the strategy and set out what your sales department will deliver to the business. It could cover total sales revenue, type of product, forecasts to help production or whatever is important. Now you have to divide this up between the team. The chapter on getting organised outlines the techniques, checklists and agreements that you need. What you cannot get from a book is the judgement essential to give the required tasks to the right people, stretch them just enough and still keep them motivated.

You will be setting the impression in the mind of each of the team of how you value them, what they are worth and where their career is going. It takes real judgement to get it right first time. Are you sure you have got it right if your plans are not immediately accepted and you have to push forcefully to get the team on board? The highest example of judgement is knowing when you have got it wrong. It happens to the best of managers. As the saying goes, keep your words soft and sweet as you never know when you have to eat them.

Engaging with the team

First, remember one essential fact; you are not one of the boys, you are the manager. It is tempting to want to be liked and there is no reason for you not to be both liked and respected. However, being liked and respected is a consequence of being seen to be on top of the job. Sales people want a manager who allows them to be successful. If you do the recruitment, strategy and organisation right, you have set the foundations for success. Engaging with the team is the way you build on the firm foundation and get the best out of each team member.

There is no typical sales person though the best do share characteristics that are discussed in chapter 5. Some are naturally optimistic, some pessimistic. Some are very open and constantly unburdening themselves. A few are secretive and tell you only the minimum. What they all need, even if they do not realise it, is regular feedback, coaching and mentoring. In chapter 8, managing the team, the typical day to day issues and problems are described. You are not there to do the selling for them. Your value is in helping them do their job better. A crucial part of your role is judging whether problems are centred on the customer or the sales person. Even the best sales people can lose sight of the bigger picture, can get bent out of shape over personalities, over estimate their abilities and under-estimate the competition. You have a right and duty to discuss selling strategy and tactics with members of the team. If you do not, you will not be able to recommend training and development to help individuals perform better. More difficult is dealing with those team members who seem to be failing. Finding out why and moving forward needs firm engagement and honest appraisals. There will be occasions when you will be wrong or make an error of judgement. If this happens over a matter of discipline or performance, the consequences can be serious.

Being the manager can all sound very dour and serious. It does not have to be – in fact if you get the basics right and team spirit is strong, the job is immensely satisfying. As the sales figures rise and individuals grow in confidence, your relationship with the team will move from plain 'the Manager' to coach and mentor. Sales meetings will be opportunities to get a real buzz into the team. Occasionally take the team off-site for the meeting and make a social event of it. Remember those who have family commitments. Trouble at home never stops at the office door.

4

Sales and Marketing – Know the Difference

Many pairings are mentioned in the same breath but are very different – husband and wife, fish and chips and so on. Sales and marketing tend to get lumped together but, unlike fish and chips, there is a perception that they can mean roughly the same thing. They are certainly not the same. They use different skills, and have different objectives. Their relative importance depends on the nature of your business. As a rule, the selling of volume consumer goods is led by marketing. Food, clothing, electrical goods and so on are promoted heavily and sold with little or no personal involvement from a sales person. High value business products or services are often sold by skilled sales people and not promoted at all or use specialist channels tightly targeting possible customers. In between are many companies with costly sales teams and a corresponding marketing budget forever trying to get the best balance and effectiveness from both. As this is a book about running a sales team, marketing will be looked at as a function to support the selling effort.

There is no shortage of books on marketing; the shelves of any good bookshop groan under the weight of them. Hence, this chapter is not a definitive guide to the theory and practice of marketing. Instead, it assumes you have a sales team, field and office based, and you want to know how marketing can help them be more effective.

In an ideal world, serious potential customers would contact your sales department because they knew about your products and could clearly see the benefits they offered. Your value proposition would be clearly articulated and made relevant to the target market. Appropriate material describing what can be purchased would be available in many forms whether paper, the internet or whatever. The sales team can advise, tailor or reassure to facilitate the sale and dismiss the competition. They will not need to spend time cold calling or selling the wrong products in the wrong markets.

This ideal world is called marketing. It can transform your company; it could also be a black hole for your money. As in many things, to get the best results, think it through. You need to know what you want from the marketing budget and then plan the spending of money. If you still think sales and marketing are similar, you have yet to hear sales people and marketers griping at each other. Sales always complain that there are not enough advertisements, nobody knows about the product or company, the product information is rubbish, the web site is out of date, etc, etc. Marketers wonder why sales people never follow up the sales leads they generate, can't sell in a market analysed and declared ripe for picking, and insist the product prices are too high when copious market research proves a very positive price advantage, taking all into consideration. There is never enough budget to satisfy everyone, so just make sure that what you do spend does count.

Here are the key things that marketing can do for your company.

- It will help you plan your products to be relevant to chosen markets.

- The size of markets and your potential business can be determined or estimated.

- Your value proposition can be analysed and, hence, clearly articulated and differentiated from the competition.

- Suitable promotional materials can be prepared.

- Your message can be distributed to customers and prospects.

- Sales leads are obtained from interested potential customers.

Marketing is not selling. You can use your sales team to collect information as they go about their business but do not expect them to do marketing. It is academic, creative and analytical in a different way from selling. Do it yourself, hire staff or use specialist companies. Your sales team should be tasked to get the business now and they cannot do this and at the same time cope with the different timescales and demands of marketing. To see how you can use marketing techniques to improve business. take the above points in turn.

- **It will help you plan your products to be relevant to chosen markets.**

You may have started in a particular market with a product but now see your growth limited by this first market. Can your product be successfully introduced to a different market? While you could hire a sales person expert in the new market, this is a high risk move unless you are absolutely sure that the product or service is acceptable. Market research can give you more information. The internet has revolutionised market research. What took days spent in trade and public libraries can now be done at your desk on the internet. Much of the information is free and, if carefully chosen, accurate. Potential customers and the key competitors can be identified. Trade associations often publish lists of members and the industry exhibitions promote participating companies.

The web gives lots of information but not always a lot of inside knowledge or wisdom. You may find out who are the biggest customers and the dominant suppliers who could be your competitors. However, what makes success and whether you have the magic ingredient could be more elusive to define. If you are not entirely sure and are hesitant to invest real money and effort cracking the market, then get expert advice. Individual consultants, specialist market research companies and similar are at hand for a fee. Doing this work is time consuming but is an investment in market knowledge. If you want to get it done, then be very specific on the deliverables. When you have a niche product, it is even more necessary to get advice on your chosen market from an expert. An alternative source of temporary help to get market or product information is to use students. Consider a short assignment fitting in between terms for a marketing or business studies student. Given that you recruited the right one, they can be economical, keen and should have computer skills. While you look at new markets, do not forget to keep on top of your current markets. It is easy to think that you have them covered and miss developments or new competitors.

At some point you decide whether to enter the market. This is where you think about selling again but, and this is important, you are not finished with marketing yet.

- **The size of markets and your potential business can be determined or estimated.**

Later in the book, the troublesome issue of setting sales targets will be looked at. You may have been in a particular market for some time and are content to set targets based on historical sales. You could be missing out with this policy. Do you know your market share? Is it going up or down? Possibly you have avoided setting targets due to the difficulty of getting them right. If growth is slow, is the problem with your market or the sales team? If you are entering a new market, is it big enough to be worth the effort. Is it expanding or contracting? Well, okay, you will never get the answers to all these questions. Sometimes though, you do need some of the answers to some of the questions. To at least get close to an accurate answer can be crucial to your business decisions.

The fundamental reason for doing market research is to develop your business. While this may be obvious with new markets, don't forget the market you are in. Business owners, managers and sales people can get increasingly blinkered over time. If the business keeps dripping in steadily, commercial awareness can get hypnotised and the company dozes in the happy valley of comfortable tedium. If it all starts to go wrong, whether it is technical change, recession or whatever, you may not notice until too late. The example of the frog is often quoted. While a frog will jump out of hot water if it accidentally and suddenly falls in, it may not notice if it is sitting in cool water that is gradually getting hotter until too late. A degree of paranoia is helpful in business so keep looking ahead, over your shoulder and behind you. That way you will not be taken by surprise.

Let us look first at overall market information. There is a mountain of data produced every year on products and markets. Government statistics, trade associations, think tanks, marketing and market consultancies churn out numbers that you can obtain for free or for a variety of charges. Whether you find anything that really helps you is a different matter. The more mainstream your business, the more likely it is that there is pertinent data available. If your segment is more niche then there will be less specific information. You can identify that a market is growing but trends within it based on factors such as technology or fashion may give you an opportunity or make entry difficult. Even declining markets can feature opportunities. This is not meant to discourage time spent on collecting data. You just need to be clear on what you can get from this kind of market research and its limitations.

While much information is free, some specialist reports will be chargeable so get a list of contents and summary before spending money. Knowing your market from outside opinion and statistical terms gives you a further context to judge the performance of your own company. It is quite possible that you are under-performing and so a fresh look at targets and the training and management of the sales team is necessary.

Do you read around your subject? There are several quality newspapers and magazines with respected business sections. At least one should be read every day. If your market and your customers are being commented on or analysed, then you need to know. While much copy from these sources can be opinionated and selective, there is some good information and feel for the sentiment in a market. Conferences and seminars should be scrutinised for possible value. If a conference will take up most of a day or more then check it out carefully. To be worthwhile it must give you knowledge that you cannot get elsewhere for free or more cheaply. Conferences are good for specialist subjects or markets. They are networking opportunities with both the speakers and other attendees. Beware the professional conference attendee; you want to meet real movers and shakers in the business. However, as companies get leaner, such people attending conferences are getting scarcer.

If you want to move into new markets, all the above applies but one piece is still missing. You have a complete picture of the chosen market but you still do not know if that market wants your specific product or service. At some point you will have to decide the next move. Are you in or out? If you are out then you believe there is no reasonable opportunity. The risk is lost business. If you want in then you need to spend money and time. The risk is that this could be wasted. Entering a new market is tricky and full of pitfalls. This book is not meant to go too deeply into marketing and so it is recommended that more specialist sources are used. From a purely sales point of view, the issue is do you invest in more sales effort or re-distribute what you have to cover the new market. As a general rule do not use sales people to do marketing. This has been mentioned earlier. Secondly do not ask sales people to do things that conflict or could result in them taking their eye off the ball. To perform best, sales people need to concentrate their efforts. Hence, asking a sales person to continue account managing an existing market and, at the same time, develop new business in a different market is not advised. Try it only if the existing market has plateaued, the sales person is not stretched and the challenge is eagerly grasped. Remember, the sales force is there first and foremost to give you business *now* so you can pay the bills. If you do not have spare capacity in the sales team and do not want to recruit just yet, look at other channels. These are discussed later in the book on alternatives to a sales force.

- **Your value proposition can be analysed and, hence, clearly articulated and differentiated from the competition.**

How often do you sit back and wonder why your customers buy your products? Perhaps more importantly, do your sales team know why they win, when they win and why they lose, when they lose? As it is unlikely that you have a perfect product for a wide range of markets at just the right price, it is reasonable to suppose that what you sell is a bit of a compromise. Having said that, most products have strengths and weaknesses and so to maximise your sales, you need to reinforce the strengths and minimise the weaknesses. Sounds simple but, like most things, you will have to do some work.

The success of your value proposition is related to suitability to the market and how it competes with rival products. The first two parts of this chapter concerned looking at the market, ensuring you have a suitable product, that the market is large enough and how well you are doing in an existing market. Now you want to ensure that the value proposition is accurately framed and articulated so that it is recognised by the market. You need to put clear water between your product and the competition. Don't believe that the sales force must already know all about this and how to do it. And don't only ask the sales force to assist in these exercises that sit on the boundary between sales and marketing. You need several different views.

How you view and articulate your product or service will impact on your sales team, promotional material, advertising, PR and product development. It will be affected by competition and to whom you are addressing in a multi-level selling situation. While you need to involve different functions in the company to contribute to this exercise, it will be the sales team who will deliver the message personally. What they say must reinforce any promotional activity or advertising. Hence, the importance of your involving all the main functions in the business. There are many techniques employed to create mission statements and brand awareness. This is best left to specialist marketing books. However, in running the sales team, the important issues are, can the team articulate the merits of the product considering the level of customer being addressed, and can the competition be effectively sidelined?

Left to themselves, the sales team can be reduced to fighting on price and responding to the advantages of the competition as described by the customer. When the sales team is being jerked around by the customer, then very soon you will be also. Using marketing techniques and people to contribute to the value proposition and understanding the competition will help to refocus the sales team on how they can win. Don't expect sweetness and light in this process. The sales people will always complain that marketing are in an ivory tower on another planet. The real state of the competition is how they find it in front of the customer. Don't be discouraged. Once you are satisfied that the product or service has been well defined and positioned against the competition ensure that the sales team believe it and use it. Collecting information on the competition is discussed in the section on reporting. Use that and information from marketing to be nimble in your response to the market. Selling is about why your product is right for the customer. If your team knows more about why the competitive products are better for the customer then you need to get to grips with why the team is on the defence.

• Suitable promotional materials can be prepared

There is a huge amount of material known as 'silent sales people'. Data sheets, newsletters, catalogues, the website and so on. They are produced to get you business so don't treat them as marketing bumf. Apart from not speaking, they do the same job as your sales team. You try to get them in front of a customer and deliver a message or image that encourages a sale.

It is tempting to dismiss as simple many of the elements of making up promotional material. You might think anyone can write a product description or a newsletter. With so much clip art available, a good looking newsletter can be knocked together in-house. This is false economy, unless you really do not have the budget get specialist help in designing all this material. There is a lot more to a web site then running up a few pages with company history and a few products. Everything that a customer gets from you, whether hand delivered or through the post, must reflect your style, image and some aspect of your message. It cannot look amateur.

Your ideal is that the material should be instantly recognisable, have impact and not end up in the bin unread. Good design is not prohibitively expensive. While you could spend millions of pounds on a complete corporate design exercise (and many corporations have) there are many competent and local publicity and design companies with more modest charges. Get the right design and you will have a clear and distinctive house style. As you have spent time on your value proposition, this can be incorporated to reinforce the effectiveness of the material. Do not under-estimate the importance of good English and the difficulty in writing it. Good-to-read English is crystal clear, unambiguous and has rhythm and flow. It is best left to people who write for a living. Sales people at all levels may have good verbal skills but rarely develop writing skills beyond the workmanlike.

Sales people feel vulnerable without good supporting literature. During a meeting, company data sheets with appropriate and easy to find data and information support the efforts of the sales person in persuading the buyer. On leaving the meeting, this company information can be left behind so continuing the sales campaign. If you use agents or distributors your promotional literature may be your only direct contact with potential customers.

Any business is now expected to have a website. Fortunately, the dot.com mania has blown over and the internet has assumed its correct place. That place is to complement your other channels to market and not to take over the world. As the business owner or sales manager, for you the issue about a website is to define what you want from it. The bottom line is that it is there to get you orders. If you have a sales team because your offering is complex and needs human intervention, then position the website to complement that. We are not dealing here with internet or direct marketing operations. They are a different subject and dealt with in a different way.

The website should have the same look and feel as the rest of the company image. As to what it should contain the following is a minimum.

- Contact details and the core message or proposition of the product or service.
- Information on the products in as much detail as sensible for a

publicly accessible site. Remember that just as you use the web for market research on your competitors they will do the same to you. Store here your data sheets, frequently asked questions, newsletters in PDF or suitable format for downloading.

- Details of agents and distributors.
- A means of requesting more information or contact.

The website address should be on all your literature and considered an integral and significant channel to your customers. Considering all the hype surrounding the internet it is astonishing how poor many websites can be. They can be under construction, out of date, difficult to read and hopeless to navigate. The trouble is, unlike advertising, direct mail and so on which ends up in front of a prospect unsolicited, you have to encourage a prospect to make an effort to access your website. Just accept this and position the site correctly within your marketing plan and budget.

- **Your message can be distributed to customers and prospects.**

If your total market is ten customers and you have ten sales people you should not have a problem in getting a message across. You are more probably like most sales managers and fret about all those potential customers who have never heard of your product and the sales team is not big enough and too busy to do anything about it. What you need is a low cost, high volume method of attracting them so the very interested ones respond and come to you. Direct mail and advertising and PR are the normal means to deliver this very desirable outcome. More recently, email, fax and text messaging has been tried. These last methods have all got bad press for various reasons so you would have to carefully consider whether to use them.

The problem with direct mail and advertising is effectiveness and success rate. Some direct mail goes to the wrong person and is binned. Some goes to the right person and is binned. Advertising is similar, in that it can just go to a mental bin. The industrialist Jo Carnegie once famously said that half of advertising is wasted, but he just did not know which half. A large part of success is accurate targeting and consistency. If you want to use these marketing methods, you should accept that it is a long haul to make it worthwhile and get steady results.

Take direct mail first. Because it is directly targeted, it should go unerringly to a specific and correct person. It is in finding this person that the skill and effort lies. You can build your own database, use the database of a direct marketing company or a combination of both. This is an important investment and represents a crucial element in your ability to have quality contact with your customers. If you do not have some form of customer database that is accurate and can be precisely analysed, then your marketing will go nowhere. It is not just a record of customer names and addresses with relevant contacts. You need to input the types of customer, what they buy, what industries they are in and so on. For contacts, you can include interests, professional and social, what type of literature they want, if at all.

It is astonishing how many companies neglect to maintain a good customer information system. Not only does it make quick and efficient contact with the customer base difficult but also analysis of the customers is next to impossible. Every contact should be recorded as they can represent potential customers. Your market research can throw up companies that may later turn into customers. With a properly structured and up-to-date customer database, you can tailor mailshots for specific products, contacts and markets. Your own database is not a distribution mechanism for junk mail. It is an integral part of your selling effort and a channel as important as the sales team. Keep adding quality contacts, update and maintain it, use it regularly, take it seriously.

Using a Direct Mail company for a selling campaign can be considered for new business or a new market. The quality of the contact list will be in the hands of the company and you will have to make your own judgements.

The design of materials for direct mail is a specialist business. Assuming that the mail ends up on a desk and does not go straight from post to pulp, there is just a moment in time to capture interest. Even if the recipient is a current customer, gaining attention is difficult. Much worse, is when the mail is of no interest and the contact is left negative. Most mails will flutter down to the bin but the best will leave the binner receptive to the next one. Work closely with the design company and plan to use direct mail in a sustained way. Integrate it into other events and times of the year when you may need to ramp up activity. You will not know if this type of customer contact is effective until you have plenty of experience and feedback.

Advertising is a whole subject in itself. It can eat money like no other marketing activity. If you have an active sales force, field and inside based, a good contact database and website, think through what advertising will give you in addition to what you already have.

- **Sales leads are obtained from interested potential customers.**

Public relations does have an image problem among the doughtier members of industry. All about airhead blondes swigging chardonnay while networking with other style-obsessed fashion victims. It seems to have nothing to do with your trade press with its concentration on grommets, chemicals and sludge disposal. However, you open up Grime Monthly when it lands on your desk and just inside is a flattering article on your chief competitor! How did they do that? You imagine your customers reading the piece and giving the rival a quick telephone call. A national broadsheet newspaper does a survey of developments in decorative products and your product or company is not mentioned. How did the others get in? It is called PR and it should not be ignored.

Every business has a story to tell. To tell it, there are any number of newspapers, magazines and journals with space to fill and readers to be attracted and retained. Recognising what is interesting about your business and writing about it in a compelling way is a special art. Getting the story in as wide a range of periodicals as possible takes more expertise. To get the most out of PR, you need to partner with a marketing or PR company and develop a good working relationship with them. It need not be expensive and it can be very effective. If you read a good piece of editorial in a trade magazine about a company or product, it has credibility and stays in the mind far longer than an advertisement.

So, how do you start? Find a PR company that has experience in your market or at least similar. Look for examples and references. If your business is screws, then an agency specialising in the film industry is no use at all. Be hard headed about this. You want awareness and leads that your sales team can turn into orders. PR may seem a bit glitzy but it is all about business. Once you have selected the agency, you need to work with them for some time. The problem is that, in the early days anyway, you will have to spend some time with them working on the stories. In fact, you are bound to say at some point that you might as well have written it yourself. This is true but, unless you write for a living, what you finish with will not have the punch and vocabulary that makes good copy.

The next issue is choosing what to write about. You are not planning a mail shot or datasheet. Put yourself in the shoes of the editor of the intended magazines or newspapers. They want circulation by offering relevant, up-to-date comment and news. Editorial space is not there to carry your latest special offer or obscure technical information. Editorial space gives you the opportunity to tell about achievements, awards, special or difficult projects, unusual uses for your products and so on. It is similar to the kind of copy you would put in your newsletter to show how capable and interesting your company or products are. Unlike your newsletter, the press release must be made attractive enough for someone else to choose to use it to enhance their periodical. This is where a PR agency is invaluable. When they know you well, they can see stories and angles you miss because you are too close to the business. They can help to make them interesting, compelling articles and advise on photographs or graphics.

When it comes to distribution of the press release, a good agency with knowledge of your industry and press can be more effective then if you try to do it yourself. Magazines vary in their approach to press releases. Some like to take some advertising as well as the PR. An agency that makes the effort to know the editors will be more successful than the blunderbuss approach.

Plan to respond to any inquires. Some magazines have a formal reply procedure. You may just get phone calls, letters or emails. Whatever you get back, ensure that you have made someone responsible for sending an acknowledgement or brochure. The response is the payoff – don't let it slip through your fingers.

Exhibitions

Exhibitions are such an established part of marketing that it is often forgotten how big a gamble they can be as measured by getting business. They can be expensive in the cost of floor space and stand design. Then there are the hidden costs. The hidden cost of exhibitions is largely in the organisation of resources and the commitment of people to staff the stand. Chose the wrong event and your prized and expensive sales team is reduced to talking to each other and contacting real punters from mobile phones in echoing exhibition halls.

There are many reasons given for going to exhibitions; most of them not valid. Here are some of them.

- We always go to Expo-Widget.
- If we do not go, customers will think we are in trouble.
- Our competitors will be there.
- Customers like to see us there.

Exhibitions are just another channel to your customers and prospects. The expense and effectiveness need to be assessed relative to all the other marketing tools available and discussed in this chapter. You need to judge the benefits of having all or part of your sales team in one place on the assumption that the people you want to see will turn up.

Why then should you go to an exhibition? There are various reasons apart from a desire to drink whisky just after breakfast because an old customer expects to be legless by lunch. Here are a few.

- It will attract all those small customers who never get a sales person to call and value the contact to continue business.

- You can demonstrate new products that would otherwise require a factory visit.
- Apart from the sales force, the senior management can be present to cement business relationships and close deals.
- Some exhibitions attract overseas visitors who may be difficult to identify by other means. It is often said that the best agents or distributors chose you rather then the other way round. An exhibition can be an excellent way to facilitate this.
- You can be as assured as possible that you will get many new prospects due to the stature of the exhibition and it will be as effective as any other marketing channel.

In your business, there could be many other deciding factors apart from or including the above. What you don't want to do is move your sales team at great expense to a draughty shed in the Midlands for a week just to collect the business cards from a few old buddies. If I am harsh about exhibitions, it is because they can be expensive and disruptive for your sales team like no other marketing activity.

On the assumption that you have chosen to go to an exhibition, you need to train the sales force and set down policies to make best use of the time. There are very good training videos and books on the subject which you would do well to acquire. Some of the following points may or may not be covered from other sources.

- Each day of the show, one person should be in charge of coverage. People need breaks for rest and to look at other stands, but the stand should never be abandoned. Don't underestimate how tiring exhibitions can be.
- Whatever happened the previous night, everyone should be on the stand on time the next morning, bright eyed and bushy tailed. They must be available to sell and should be able to sell from opening to close.
- All should have formal name badges, business cards and a means to take notes or other customer information. If you do not exchange and record mutual business interests, you are wasting your time.

- Have a plan on how to have business meetings. Design meeting rooms into the stand or have other arrangements.
- Train your sales staff on how to separate serious punters from regiments of exhibition goers who collect datasheets, free pens and want to reminisce on something from the archive.
- Think carefully on what food and drink you want on the stand. If in doubt have a bottled water supply and leave it at that.

They are lots more points I could add. The central point is that the exhibition is a serious selling opportunity and not a day out from the office. If it goes well, there are few other opportunities where your sales team will have a supply of well-qualified punters queuing to talk business. Back them up with a well designed stand, good graphics and exhibits to talk about. Employ a specialist company and design with an eye to reusing as much as possible for future events.

Seminars and conferences

These contact points with your customers all have their place. Do not under estimate the task of setting them up and the need for quality in what may be regarded as low cost events.

Seminars

Seminars are useful in complex or fast moving environments. They can be held either at your premises or in regional locations and are usually to maintain contact with ongoing customers. Speakers can be drawn from your own company and selected complementary businesses or consultants. Think of the seminar as a way to consolidate business relationships. Potential customers could be attracted but this is a low pressure selling opportunity. A high profile main speaker would give the event more credibility and attract more senior contacts. Seminars to existing customers are simple to organise and cheap to run. If you provide good coffee, decent nibbles at lunch and quality speakers, then your customer relationships can only improve.

Conferences

Having a stand at a conference sounds like a good idea. You can make an intelligent guess at the type of delegate and how many. The speakers on the programme can indicate the quality and attractiveness of the event. The cost of stand space can be modest and no one expects the stand itself to be a monument. So, it can be cheap and effective, an ideal combination. Unfortunately the reality can be different and it is best to build into your plans the dynamics of these events. Delegates turn up to hear the speakers and network with their mates. At registration they drink coffee and see who else is there. If you are lucky, they will poke their heads round the associated exhibition and note to pop in later. The first break comes and everyone is gasping for a coffee and stands in a queue. If it is a long break, you may get a few delegates drifting into the exhibition. Unfortunately these are the guys no one wants to talk to. At the lunch break, most disappear to feed but this is the prime occasion to meet them. You hope the break is long enough to allow both feeding time and exhibition visiting. The afternoon break is similar to the morning. With a one-day conference, you have to rely on delegates not wanting to get home early after the last speaker. A two-day or longer conference does give the delegates time to do the exhibition before the conference dinner.

The problem with conferences is getting the prime prospects to your stand when there are many other diversions. The best way to make your stand a first call for the delegates is to have a speaker in the main conference. Failing this, discuss with the organisers how much time the delegates will have to visit the exhibition and how the organisers can encourage them. With a limited number of delegates, you could stoop to free gifts or a draw based on obtaining business cards. At the most extreme your sales team could be staring at space for 80% of the time and unable to cope when the action starts. It may seem drastic but consider not having any senior sales people on the stand but use a junior or internal sales person to give out information and take names. Add a product specialist to talk details which may suit the typical conference delegate. Afterwards get hold of the conference delegate list to mail the ones who got away.

Good marketing will make your sales team more productive. Not only will they spend more time with serious punters but will be more motivated by the better image of the company or product. Unless your business is strongly marketing driven, many of the services required can be bought in as required. Once you have a sales strategy, integrate marketing closely and carefully. Done well, the result will be formidable.

5

Salespeople? Who Are They?

The stereotype salesmen are pictured as glib talking, smart dressing, ruthless and a moral vacuum. Barely under control of the company, they stalk the country in search of their prey. In the past, the salesman of legend sold vacuum cleaners, then double glazing, more recently, utilities, particularly gas and electricity. The tactics employed reached the pages of the tabloids where self-righteous venom was spat at the knaves and rogues. A company spokesman would always say that the offending salesman had been fired and the like would never happen again. During the pensions mis-selling scandal, one company stated that its entire sales force would be re-trained.

Strange isn't it how particular industries are hit by selling scandals? Can it be that sober, honest, 'play it fair' pillars of industry are smitten, to their surprise, by rogue sales teams? Do these charlatans sneak into venerable companies and then wreak havoc for their own personal gain? Are the boardrooms of these companies unfortunate victims. I suggest not. The sales force of a company is a reasonable reflection of that company's ethos and ethics. If the sales force is a modern Mogul hoard sweeping all in front of it, then you can be sure they are paid and encouraged to do just that.

When you recruit sales people, you will get what you are looking for. The problem is what *are* you looking for? Selling skills are often not fully understood, so identifying them when you are not a sales specialist can be difficult. Even sales managers with some experience can be misled as old perceptions persist. Time then to analyse that slippery character, the sales person.

In a previous chapter the image and role of sales was examined. It was seen that the role was very complex and with a heavy emphasis on personal skills. However, there are no relevant qualifications such as a degree or similar. Because much of the work involves interpersonal skills, it is difficult to be analytical in the relationship between the output, such as orders, with input, such as the sales person's effectiveness and effort. With marketing, the effort is very visible, brochures, advertising, mail campaigns, etc. The results can be measured in leads, market awareness and so on. With this in mind how can the really important characteristics of good sales people be identified? If it is possible and done as accurately as possible, you will get the sales force you want. Do not accept the image of sales described in chapter 2. You can get professional, successful people with integrity if you set your standards high and identify the type of person you want.

Consistently, successful sales people have a number of characteristics that set them apart from the average or uneven performers. Here are the important ones.

Sensitivity
Self-discipline
Positive work-rate
Analytical ability
Active listening
Persuasiveness
Problem solving skills
Creativity
Seeking closure
Tenacity
Integrity
Team working
Technical skills

High performance sales people will show many of the above and indicate the vital characteristics very strongly. It may seem a long list but, don't forget, it is a complex job. I have left out passion. It is both too nebulous and dangerous an emotion to seek for one aspect of a company function. Remember, you are not looking for entrepreneurs here. You want an important job done well, not your company dancing to an individual's tune. In fact, of the successful sales people I have met, few had ambitions to run a company or go outside more senior positions within sales. If you spot that a sales person starts looking more like an entrepreneur, then it's time for a career conversation before it turns dangerous.

I have not mentioned money, bonuses or commission at all. So far. Money will not make a bad sales person into a good sales person. Also, what you pay and how you do it must feed back to your business plan and not be seen to be just a mechanism to satisfy individual needs.

Let us look at the characteristics and skills listed above in more detail.

Sensitivity

I recognised this several years ago as a key attribute of the very best sales people. It may seem surprising as many believe that the love of earning loads of money was the key driver for the best staff. I have come to know better and recognise the effectiveness of sales people with sensitivity.

By sensitivity I do not mean warm, big hearted, huggy people who cry for others. I mean people who have an acute sense of other people's body language, emotions, needs and anxieties. Also, the effect of their own words and appearance. One salesman I knew, with an abundance of sensitivity, always carried his briefcase in his left hand before a meeting so his right hand would be dry and cool for when he shook hands with his client. Highly developed sensitivity will allow better judgements to be made on the progress of a sale. Difficult negotiations will be eased. The sensitive sales person will know when to be tough, when to ease off, how and when to coax useful information out of a contact. Sensitivity is not about smooth talking or glibness. It has more to do with accurate observations and listening. The sensitive sales person will detect tensions, pressures, hidden lines of authority and the political and emotional barriers to progress.

This is a skill that is not easily taught in a formal sense. It comes from experience and use of other skills such listening and negotiating. You can recognise it in a sales person because he or she will appear to be always one jump ahead of what is happening.

Self-discipline

Self-discipline is not the same as work-rate. We'll look at work-rate later but the two attributes are at the heart of many business owners' and managers' anxieties over sales people. Are they doing what they are supposed to do and is their nose firmly on the grindstone?

Self-discipline is doing what you know you have to do without being told. Selling is not all about having lunch. Much of the work is routine, can be boring and, sometimes, emotionally difficult. It is easy to call a customer and say the delivery will be early. Making that call when the delivery is delayed, maybe not for the first time, takes self-discipline and preparation. Part of self-discipline is personal organisation. Making time to do the things that really need to be done, easy or difficult.

Employing sales people who are not self-disciplined is hard work for the manager or business owner. They are the channel to the customer and if issues are not communicated and nettles grasped, then customer satisfaction tumbles.

Many of the sales tools and much training for sales try to address this issue. The management problem is that the sales person is frequently out of the office (who knows where), is in sporadic contact with management (perhaps deliberately), and problems from customers appear to come out of thin air. The normal answer is to produce formal disciplines based on reports of activities together with customer details. This kind of feedback is important anyway, but you should know why you are doing it. If it is in order to know more about the sales person than the customer, then there is a problem.

Positive work-rate

How many times have you heard someone described as having lots of energy, partly as an excuse for, say, lack of experience? I mention this because work-rate and energy can be similar in effect but they are not the same thing at all. Work-rate is the speed that someone uses to get through the essentials of the job. In fact, a high work-rate and self-discipline are probably the two most important characteristics of consistently successful salespeople. To be the very best, more is needed – sensitivity and creativity in particular. But, for consistent and reliable sales and a high customer satisfaction, work-rate and self-discipline are 80% of what matters.

Don't be fooled by long working hours. The sales person may have other reasons for not wanting to go home. Sales people with good work-rates never waste time. They rarely hang around the coffee machine or have their lunch break in the pub. While they will take breaks, they will be taken, like everything else, with a snappy precision. You will get few customer complaints about these people and you can relax that if it needs to be done then it is being done.

Low work-rate can be disguised by high energy or high activity. If you are not sure, ask such people if they are busy. The high work-rate people will say they are but they'd like to help. The low work-rate will also say they are busy but probably add that they have too much work and ask if there is a problem. Low work-rate but high energy or activity usually highlights a need for training. They just may not know what they should be doing or what is important. Low work-rate and low activity is usually terminal in a sales job unless they have a significant other skill.

The very best sales people I have known all had very high work-rates and self-discipline. Most of them could be described as obsessive in their diligence to leave nothing undone that would imperil an order or affect customer satisfaction. These top sales people had other abilities as well that showed as and when needed, but it was in work-rate and self-discipline that they excelled. These people are easy to spot – they are as demanding of their management as they are of themselves.

Analytical ability

Sales people get deluged with data and information. Many have more opportunities than they can handle, in theory that is. Unless you are able or wish to direct your sales people in a very precise way, you will have to leave it to them. It is in the area of new business or where a sales person has too big a territory or apparent business opportunities that analytical skills are important. Collecting data is not too difficult as much that is needed is published on the web. Knowing what to collect, how much of it and then using it knowledgeably takes experience and knowledge. Sales people looking after large accounts should carefully dissect the annual report and accounts for opportunities.

The best sales people sniff out opportunities by a combination of experience and solid legwork. This skill overlaps with marketing and was a role known as Business Development. It is now a title commonly given to new business sales people. It might be safer to assume that a task that requires much analytical effort should be given to marketing. The good sales people will do it anyway.

Active listening

There is a place for the silver-tongued talker but for most sales roles that place is in popular mythology. Asking the right questions and listening carefully to the answers is key to understanding where you stand on getting that order or whether you should move on. This section is headed active listening for a reason. Listening is a skill, not just to understand what is being said but also to encourage disclosure and openness. In many ways, it is part of sensitivity, knowing how to draw out information that could be vital to knowing how to plan the sales campaign. Active listening is not the same as the use of silence. Silence is used sometimes to force a decision and can be threatening. Active listening can gain friends and confidence.

Asking questions is not particularly difficult; you can prepare for that in advance. Getting good answers gives the raw material on which account plans are made and a proposal moulded to the needs of the customer. Many a lost sale analysis has thrown up an objection that no one remembers. Ask the question, listen carefully to the answer. Many customers do not give totally truthful answers. The unscrupulous salesmen of legend are often only outdone by some villainous buyers. They will play one sales person off against another and mislead to gain advantage. The sales person needs to have many contacts, ask many questions and carefully analyse the answers. Knowledge gives advantage.

Unlike many other sales skills, the practiced active listener is easy to spot. Afterwards you may have a feeling that you gave too much away; too late, it's gone.

Persuasiveness

To be persuasive must be an obvious characteristic of a sales person. Why was this not put first? Largely because this is a skill that can only be used frequently when all the other important attributes are there. For persuasion to be credible, the sales person must, first, be in front of the customer as regularly as possible. Then, having listened carefully, be able to be analytical about the solution and approach. Being articulate is often confused with being persuasive. Persuasion is being articulate with a defined purpose. Also, beware of mere sophistry. It is here that sales people get their reputation for glibness alongside politicians.

Problem solving skills

I was in a large multi-national company and asked a colleague what he thought was the role of sales. He drew a large square to represent the company. Within the square he drew several circles to represent company departments such as engineering, contracts and so on. All the space in between the square and the circles was sales in his opinion. There was a lot of truth in this. If the sales person represents the company to the customer, then he represents all the departments and the interaction between them.

If there is an issue with a customer, the sales person hears it first and is expected to sort it. Often it is not a sales issue, sometimes not even a fault of the company but a frisson within the customer. Whatever the reason, the sales person catches it first.

Problem solving can be a difficult area for sales people. The real causes of problems with customers can lie very deep. Only good questioning and knowledge of the customers can led to solutions. The difficulty for management or business owners is that the sales person may only pick up the complaint at face value. Common complaints are product unreliability, poor servicing, prices too high and so on. The unskilled sales person could report back and just criticise the relevant departments to protect the revenue from the customer. The result for management includes increased costs and internal frictions. It could be that the complaints are justified. It could also be true that the customer has inadequate training for their staff and so mis-uses the products.

Many sales people are uncomfortable with these interdepartmental tasks. They may see them as a diversion from the main job of getting orders. If your business is complex and account management important, then a problem-solving sales person could be vital. If these skills are lacking, the business owner may end up solving the problem, and maybe too late.

Creativity

Genuinely creative people are rare. They are just as rare in the selling profession. 80% of successful selling is hard work, self discipline and work rate as mentioned before. You can form a very successful sales team on these assets alone. There is more scope for creativity in marketing than sales with its role in message and image making. However, creative sales people are formidable operators. They are most likely to be spotted when working for the competition. A deal, apparently 'in the bag' goes to a competitor. The customer is questioned as to why the other product or service was chosen. Among the reasons given is one that satisfies a need never mentioned before. This is puzzling, but it is clear that you have been out-sold. Unknown to your sales person, the potential customer had been asked to look at the purchase in a completely different way.

Creative sales people can look at a sales campaign and plan it to outwit the competition. They can encourage the prospect to explore new needs and show how they can be satisfied by a benefit of the product or service. This capability to think outside the box is the key to the creative sales person. They will never compete head to head with a rival but try to make themselves as different as possible. Many selling situations result in very similar products or services being pitched at the prospect. Here, creative sales people are worth all the money needed to retain them. They are usually identified by their questioning which is unusually wide ranging. They like to spot a need outside the project in hand. Solve that with the same product and they get the sale while the opposition are left scratching their heads.

Seeking closure

This usually means closing techniques. Closing techniques have acquired an almost mythical status with the general public. These fearsome tricks are thought to effortlessly extract orders from the sturdiest sceptics. There are many about, some with specific names, like the half nelson, but they fit into a very few types. The main ones are either implying the offer is accepted and only the details need to be dealt with, or suggesting some dire consequence if a signature is not given immediately.

There are two problems with relying on closing techniques. The first is, unless you are dealing with an unsophisticated section of the general public, most professional buyers know all the standard tricks. Every closing technique has an equal and opposite buyer's negotiating position. The second is that sales people who hone their closing techniques are basically poor at asking for the order. This may seem strange but, in talking to top sales people, rarely do they mention closing techniques. If they had to resort to these kinds of tricks, they would have felt that they had badly managed the whole sales campaign.

The top sales people seek closure at the earliest moment possible in the sales cycle. We will look at the sales cycle later but, for now, accept that a process has to happen before an order can be given. Good sales people will know that and, ideally, structure the campaign such that an order is a final and inevitable consequence of actions. At the right point, a confident sales person will ask for the order without smoke, mirrors or a mysterious form of words.

Good sales people will do what are known as trial closes. These are used for a variety of reasons but essentially to test how close they are to a decision or if there are problems that have not been addressed. They can winkle out issues by making the prospect understand that an order is expected so any concerns that need to be addressed should be brought out. Used well, trial closes push some responsibility onto the prospect to be open about what they really want and when they want it.

Many good sales people falter at closure. After a long campaign, asking for the order is the crunch point. Handled badly, it can delay or lead to failure. Unfortunately, in both professional and private life, some people just cannot make a decision. These people need to be pressed. The good closer will politely but firmly move the prospect to a decision.

Tenacity

During the life cycle of a product or service, there will be periods of being uncompetitive, over-priced, poorly made, delivered late or plain unsuitable for the market. Someone has to tell the customer and that someone is the salesperson. Added to that are buyers who delight in making a sales person jump through hoops before releasing the order, or give the order to a competitor, leaving the sales person to start again somewhere else. Whatever happens with a company or a customer, the sales person is affected and that is why tenacity is needed. Resilience, determination and stoicism could be added but tenacity includes the ability to hang in despite all.

Taken to extremes, tenacity can be counter-productive, leading the sales person to hang on to lost causes and lose a sense of proportion. Without it though, a sales person will not plough through the difficult parts of the job and the setbacks which are part and parcel of getting business. This is not about being thick skinned. Thick-skinned sales people can build up dissatisfactions in the customer which later come back to hinder future business. The tenacious sales person takes the long view and sees some pain now leading to rewards later.

The tenacious sales person is admirable but not suitable for all sales jobs. If you need business now, particularly if your company is young, you need a skilled picker of low-hanging fruit. If the long view on a sales prospect is longer than your line of credit, then you will be bust. But, for long and complex sales or account management, tenacity is valuable. Tenacious sales people can be identified when you ask them about a difficult sale. If it sounds like the retreat from Moscow but ending in victory, then you have a prize example.

Integrity

Integrity and sales are not normally mentioned in the same sentence. Many believe that to sell, some distortion of the truth is required. Let's be clear now about this. If it is necessary to lie about a product to sell it, then the problem is deeper than the sales person. If the sales person attempts to mislead or deceive a customer, then it is a straightforward matter of discipline *and* a management problem.

Selling is a personal skills business. There is emotion involved even if battle-hardened street warriors say they've been there, done it and got the order, bloody but unbowed. In asking the customer to buy something, the sales person is saying 'believe me'. In many ways, sales people are selling themselves. The best sales people, or, at least, the ones you want to employ, want to believe in what they are selling. They also want to honour commitments. If a sales person gives a delivery time to a customer, then it is painful to have to call back if the promise cannot be held. Not only does the customer give the sales person, as the company representative, a hard time but there is always implied that the sales person misled in the first place. To build up steady business, a sales person needs to create trust. Trust and integrity move selling from being a confrontation between buyer and seller upwards towards partnership. Sales people need integrity. It drives their self-esteem. They need to feel that what they say has the whole company behind them. When they sell the product, they are selling themselves as well.

Of course things go wrong. Despite best intentions, deliveries will be late, a service won't arrive on time and so on. Managing expectations is part of integrity. Integrity is similar to honesty in that it is about openness. If the delivery will be late then making that call, in advance, giving a good explanation, plus the remedial action adds to the sales person credibility. So, integrity is not so much about saintliness but doing the right thing, even though it is tough. A word of warning about employing sales people with a sense of integrity; they usually demand the same from their employers.

Team players

The above characteristics are not exhaustive for sales people but they lie at the core of the best in the business. There is a further differentiation of sales people that can be important. As in all categorisations, nothing is completely cut and dried, however, it is possible to identify the individual contributor from the team player. Both have their place but they are very different.

It is fashionable to emphasis team building as essential to the modern company. It certainly has its place and in some functions it is vital. But, before sending your sales team on a survival weekend on Dartmoor with three matches and a Swiss army knife, just think it through. Unless you are operating a call centre type selling operation, your team may only meet sporadically at the coffee machine. In sales, a team player is someone who works across company functions to bring together a solution or solve a company problem. However, many sales people are individual contributors who prefer to deliver sales, stay out of the office and play golf with the customer rather than a colleague. Both, in their way are very suitable sales people.

A few words about sales people who you want to be team players. If the responsibility of delivering a solution or maintaining a relationship with the customer rests on the sales person, then, really you don't want a team player. You want someone to deliver a result and the sales person is really the team leader; players play, leaders deliver. Sales people offering complex solutions or dealing with complex customers have to be skilled in forming virtual, multi-disciplinary teams. Getting a disparate group of, say, engineers, contracts, admin and finance people lined up behind a bid and agreeing what it should say is a huge task. Some people love it and see the work involved in getting a large amount of the company resources behind their project as very satisfying. Some don't and dislike intensely having to rely on other people to do what they think is their job. Well, it's horses for courses. A large team may well have team players and individual contributors all delivering the orders. Just remember that, when recruiting or handing out accounts, you correctly identify the right people.

The sales team leader may or may not be the archetypal social whirlwind, always down the pub making friends. If they are, you may be looking at a team player. The team leader knows who can help get the order and builds the team with that in mind. The team leader is above all an internal sales person, able to convince those necessary that, by giving backing, they are backing a winner. The resulting win will enhance the reputations off all involved.

Technical skills

We've all heard it: 'Damn salesman didn't know what he was talking about!' Conversely, is the pleasure of finding a sales person who does know the subject. So, no argument – get someone who understands the technology, service or whatever. Well … maybe. A sales person is employed to sell and that involves a range of skills that may have much or nothing to do with the actual product. Broadly, a sales person needs to know the benefits of what he or she is selling and the possible impact on the customer. Don't be mesmerised by a possible sales person who knows all about the product, particularly if it is complex. You may simply have a closet techie.

There are a number of situations where you may need more than minimal product knowledge. If you will not be able to give office support or a specialist to accompany your dedicated road warrior, then the product needs to be simple or the sales person has to know the subject. Be candid about this before hiring any sales person. Some sales people can be hungry for resource and the lack of expected back-up can be terminal.

Legal aspects

In some industries, particularly financial, qualifications and certifications are mandatory or desirable. Even if not, sales people need to know commercial law. Certain applications can be high risk. If you may be operating in this area, your sales people need to be able to identify and quantify the technical and commercial risk. Considering the situations a sales person can get you in, it is astonishing how little legal training most sales professionals have.

Complex solutions

If your business is based on a complex application, product or solution, then you may already have technical back-up. However, the sales person may have to make the final judgement on a deal that covers both technical and commercial considerations. The sales person may have to understand the technical considerations sufficiently to balance them against the customer needs and risk. It is very easy to falter in a sale or cloud the real issues by responding to concerns by the specialists that may not be relevant or be overstated in a particular situation. The sales person may have to have enough technical confidence to push through a decision or proposal despite reservations or even opposition from parts of the company. You may well find yourself forced to back your sales person against another part of the company. Have you recruited someone you can trust enough to do that?

If you get sales staff who can get a tick in the box in all the above categories, then you have employed true sales professionals. Most sales people, even successful ones, fall short in some areas. Concentrate on the first three, particularly self-discipline and work-rate, as these are the basic building blocks. Training can help to fill in the gaps and give greater confidence.

6

Recruitment

Recruitment is a difficult business for even the simplest of jobs. Employing staff is a major investment, and for many companies, people are more expensive than capital equipment. With a capital investment, the costs, payback and function can be well defined. Hence the appeal of robots. People are a different matter, even for a well defined job, such as a lorry driver. While the job can be described and costed, the temperament of the driver can wreck the plans – and the truck.

Much work has been done on testing to complement the standard interview. Psychometric testing is popular as it seeks to determine the basic nature of a candidate without the candidate being able to influence the result. For many simple to define jobs, this technique is probably useful. The problem for sales recruitment is that candidates can have very different natures yet be very proficient in the job. The bottom line is that you will not really know what you have recruited until the new sales person is more than a month into the job.

Sales recruitment is particularly stressful. You will take someone you barely know and let them loose on your customers to represent everything you stand for. The success of your business may depend solely on their endeavours, honest and energy. But, you will rarely see them and they could be playing golf when supposedly getting you orders. The relationship between a business owner and a sales person can be more fraught than with any other employee.

Is it possible then to reduce the risk to a point where you stand a chance of getting the employee you want? The answer is yes, given care and diligence. The following does make a number of assumptions. It assumes that you are recruiting for an honest company which values sound, clean business and long-term customer satisfaction. If you want a pack of wolves and have only a short business plan, then different rules apply that are not covered here.

For any sales role, there are a few core personal characteristics. These were described in the previous chapter on sales people. When recruiting there are two that are essential, self-discipline and work-rate. Without these two essentials, all other desirables will be wasted. To know what else is desirable it is necessary to carefully define the job on offer.

Define the role

There are a few key aspects to the role that need to be identified immediately. This will help when framing an advertisement or briefing a recruitment company. For specialist roles, there will be specific attributes, but the following will get you 90% of the way.

(a) Will it be an internal sales (office based) position?
(b) Is it a field sales job or 'on the road'?
(c) If on the road, local office based or home based?
(d) Predominately new business or existing accounts?
(e) Are qualifications mandatory?
(f) Is experience of a particular industry necessary?
(g) Is the market aggressively competitive?
(h) Is the market consultative in approach?

Let us look at the above in detail. The object is to arrive at a profile of the ideal candidate for the job.

Will it be internal or on the road?

These are basically the two issues of cost and effectiveness. Keeping a sales person on the road can cost twice as much as an internal sales position. Not only are the costs higher but also the call rate is lower. Managing an internal sales person is more simple, effectiveness quickly judged and the role tightly structured. The growth of telesales indicates the possibilities with this low-cost model. Even the most technical of products or markets can benefit from an internal sales function. There is more about internal or on-the-road sales in the chapter on making the team. For now, the issue is that for a field sales person, more thought will have to go into the choice of candidate.

Local or remote?

If the territory is large or remote from where management is based, then the sales person will have to operate for long periods in some isolation. Home working is the normal solution and the growth of broadband networking mean that home or mobile working is technically satisfactory. However, the issues are rarely technical but personal. If you have not managed people who work from home then you need to get your mind around the issues. There is both the problem of management of external sales people and the isolation that can be very negative for them. If you do not trust your remote sales people and they feel neglected, then there are the ingredients for trouble.

New business or existing accounts?

Most sales roles involve both new and existing business. Even with existing accounts, the business will need to be developed further. It is tempting for sales people to just let the business roll and only reach for the low hanging fruit. However, the natural new business specialist is a different person from what could be called the Account Manager. This will be discussed in the section on making the team and, when recruiting, it is very important to get it clear up front if new business is a priority. A good new business sales person will cost more than an existing account manager.

Qualifications?

Some qualifications are mandatory for doing the job, particularly in the financial services industry. There is no getting away from this. Just make sure you are up to speed on the latest regulations and the bodies authorised to issue the qualifications.

Outside of the mandatory qualifications, there are probably few that are essential to the job of being a sales person. There are no degrees in sales and don't think that an MBA is a substitute. But, this definitely does not say that a degree from the university of life will do. Other than the most simple of sales situations or telesales from a script, selling is a complex business. The sales person will need a high intellectual capital to be consistently successful. A degree in engineering clearly would be helpful for selling in the engineering industry but, even where a direct subject degree is not obvious, get the best formal qualifications possible. Sales people have to absorb information quickly, understand and judge the possibilities, and plan a response. Never underestimate the intelligence required to sell effectively. If you do, you'll learn the hard way; your company will be outsold.

Is experience of an industry necessary?

Ideally, yes. But unless there are very good reasons, do not put this qualification on a pedestal. Good sales people learn the dynamics of a market quickly and selling is person to person whatever the industry. Having said that, there are some points that could be important.

The public sector is different in attitude to the private sector. Even with new financial pressures in the public sector, the motivations and ambitions of many of the staff are different from that of the private sector. Different, not less – and, in many ways, less easy to understand. If your business is mostly public sector and at senior levels, then it would be wise to get public sector experience. Many public sector deals are long and complicated so screwing up by inexperience could be costly.

Another reason to buy industry experience is if you want to move into a new market and you have no existing expertise in the company. Hiring an expert can kick-start your launch. Beware of potential sales people holding fat contact books. You can buy lists of contacts for most industries so you still want someone who can demonstrate they can close business for you.

Is the market competitive or consultative?

Do you want a street fighter or a strategist? There are markets where the sales management is obsessed about the competition and has every reason to be so. In these markets the sales person takes into account that everything they say will be taken to the competition and trashed. Success requires a little healthy paranoia and tremendous resilience. Management of these sales people can also be stressful but, if that is the market, then take it on the chin. Any thing less may mean failure. Consultative selling based on knowledge, trust and some gravitas, is different in style but requires the same energy. It's just wise not to mix them up.

Start the search

Somewhere, out there, is your ideal candidate and he or she is probably working for someone else. How do you make your contact? There are a number of ways, all having advantages and disadvantages.

Phone a friend

Schemes to reward employees who recommend potential candidates are popular and successful. You can offer a substantial prize and still do it at a fraction of the cost of a recruitment company. You will get a known quantity and an employee is less likely to recommend an anti-social, incompetent disaster area. A sales person is likely to recommend another sales person who is in competition, so there is the possibility of strengthening your own team and weakening the competition. While the quality of candidate may be high the number are limited so you may quickly exhaust this route.

Recruitment companies

Recruitment is an aggressively competitive business. When you accept a candidate from one of them and get the bill, you will see why. There are also some recruitment specialists where, once you have made contact, you will never shake off a persistent, well disciplined, telesales campaign to keep in touch on your recruitment needs. There are three good reasons to use these companies. First, you have no time yourself for a complex, time consuming job. Second, it is possible that your ideal candidate is satisfied where they are and will never read a job advertisement. This will need a candidate search. Lastly, you may need anonymity if you do not want the market or competitors to know that you are recruiting.

The recruitment business covers a wide market from individuals servicing a niche industry to multi-disciplinary consultancies with offices around the world. There are few ways to tell the incompetent from the geniuses and, in many ways, they resemble estate agents. However, unlike estate agents, it is common to hold back a sizable proportion of the fee until the candidate has been in the job for some agreed time. If your road warrior turns out to be a fugitive and gets the sack during this probation period, then the agency forfeits the balance of the fee. Recruitment can be a time-consuming task with many disappointments and *caveat emptors* (just like buying a house) and good agencies can take a lot of work and strain off you. But it will cost. Typical of services are:

- job analysis
- job description
- advertisement creation
- search
- interview and screening
- verification of CVs
- psychometric testing
- candidate database.

Most managers or business owners recruiting staff usually approach recruitment agencies with one of two requests; can you find a candidate meeting a certain criteria or, do you have a suitable candidate on the database. If you choose this route you can skip the rest of this chapter until the interview.

Do it yourself

You will save money compared with using a recruitment agency but the downside is the time that the whole process will absorb. Also, unless you want to become a headhunter, you will probably only attract those who are actively seeking a change of job.

After designing your advertisement, suitable media can be chosen and the size and frequency of insertions planned. Hopefully, a satisfactory response will lead to a short-list of suitable candidates. First interviews identify a possible ideal employee and a good alternative. Follow up interviews confirm the choice and the offer is accepted. Simple. It should always be just like that but real life takes over at some point and you see why recruitment agencies are popular.

Recruit from within

A very tempting option. You get a known quantity and the employee knows all about the company and products. Just remember that if your new sales person comes from a different function, he or she may have few of the key skills essential for success. There is also the issue of filling the new vacancy in the engineering, contracts or whatever department.

It is vital to understand why recruitment from within seems attractive. It is possible that you inherently distrust sales people with the attendant management problems of dealing with staff you do not see regularly. Promoting someone you trust overcomes this. You may also want to show that career progression is possible and to be encouraged. If the product is complex then getting someone technically competent is tempting as it is often believed that customers want to deal with someone 'who knows what they are talking about'.

Employees in some functions may see sales as a more glamorous and lucrative career option. Company car, travel, business lunches all give sales a mystique not available to many other jobs. Anyway, it's so easy, travel around, chat to customers, give a quote and the orders roll in. A sizable proportion of employees promoted into sales jobs become disillusioned as the reality of relentless pressure and activity take their toll.

Recruitment from within must be as painstaking and methodical as with an outside candidate. In some ways it is more difficult. With no track record in a sales function, you will be looking for potential with little to go on for the essentials of a sales job. If it does not work out, the resolution can be emotionally draining. Even if you have the right candidate, you will need to give training and give time for the new sales person to be fully effective. Recruiting from within is not a quick fix. But, done effectively it can be an excellent way to motivate employees and get loyalty.

Going fishing, part 1 – prepare the bait

You have analysed the job and issued a description. You now consider the various options on how to contact the market. If you have started a 'phone a friend' scheme just wait for any results. Perhaps you have decided you do not have the skills or time and now are looking for a recruitment agency. Depending on the type of agency and how much you want them to do, you can skip many of the next steps. Don't forget though that the final decision will be yours even if you don't get involved until the shortlist or recommendation. You may have a possible internal candidate. If so, go straight to interviewing. However, if you do not have anyone lined up or being contacted, then you need to prepare for advertising.

Advertising

Job advertisements for sales people tend to be cliché-ridden for the good reason that a cliché communicates fast. They also fall into two groups, the content-free hype and the mini job description. If you are not too sure of the type of person you need and want to test the market, then the content-free hype will get many replies. It is assumed here that some thought has gone into recruitment and you know what you are looking for. If not this book has been wasted.

The object of the advertisement is to solicit as few as possible apparently well qualified and suitable candidates. Too many and you will spend all your time sifting through no hope CVs or CVs you cannot be sure of. Organising and conducting interviews is a time-consuming task, so do not make it more onerous. To succeed, your advertisement needs to be specific, eye catching and beguiling. You are trying to attract people who are already looking – but do not expect them to read carefully every ad. The first three lines are crucial if you want the rest of the text to be read.

There are any number of opinions on how to do a job advertisement. However, unless you want to be wacky or clever, the following is suggested.

First line. Title of job and market or industry. Sales Engineer, Salesman or Sales Representative are less common now. Unless you want to project a slightly dusty image, use one of the newer titles. Sales Executive is just about acceptable though the word executive is getting slightly tacky. There is a lot of image and self esteem in this role so anything with the word 'manager' is good. Sales Account Manager, Regional Sales Manager and so on all increase the prestige of the job. Some titles have migrated from jobs that were really marketing. Business Development Manager and Business Manager that had a strong marketing focus are commonly used for purely sales jobs. The former is a new way to describe new business selling. After the job title, I would suggest stating the industry. This is not essential but some markets, such as financial sales, have essential requirements and you may need to send an early signal to them.

Second line. Salary and benefits. It is unlikely you will attract a sales person just by their love of your product. Not impossible, just unlikely. The second line should give the compensation for the best possible candidate and any attractive extras such as share options and a quality car.

Third line. Brief description of company. Actually this can be several lines. Depending on the type of person you are looking for, you can emphasis growth, stability, market position or any thing else germane to the role. The idea is to create an image of the type of company the ideal candidate would want to work for. For new business, perhaps emphasise the innovation and growth achieved; for existing business, the number of customers.

Forth line. Description of role. A paragraph or several bullet points. Do not overdo this but remember that you are still selling at this point. Use action words, for instance, 'sell to banking industry' is not as dynamic as 'capture significant share of banking market'.

Fifth line. Ideal candidate. Here is where you can cut down the no-hope candidates to a minimum. Qualifications and experience can be spelled out with as much emphasis as necessary.

Ending. Who and how to contact, with any closing date. You can ask the candidate to request an application form or invite CVs. The advantage of an application form is that you can more easily compare candidates and seek the information you are interested in. This is not recommended for sales people. You want to know how they present themselves in what is effectively a cold call situation. Let them start selling by leaving the candidate with the choice of how approach you.

What medium?

At this stage you have the ideal profile of candidate, described them in the advertisement and now you have to catch their eye. Depending on the job and seniority there are four broad media categories:

- local publications
- national publications
- trade journals
- the internet.

Local publications

In general, these are good for less senior appointments. It may be useful in some instances to ensure that the candidates live locally and may be relevant for an internal sales position.

National publications

Good for senior appointments and spreading the net. More expensive than local publications and could generate too big a response. Also the advertisement could get lost in among the big corporate advertisements. If you are looking for remotely based staff but are not too bothered about exact location, a national publication is best. General publications are useful if good candidates could come from a variety of working backgrounds.

Trade journals

For some professions there are journals that are always read by job hunters. Teaching is a good example where The Times Education Supplements carry most of the advertising. If you must recruit from within the industry or market and there is a respected journal, then there is no choice. However, publication is often monthly which can delay the recruitment process. Also, you may not want to so directly alert your competitors to the fact that you are recruiting.

The internet

Many of the serious national publications also use the internet. For internet-only recruitment, the potential candidate must be actively searching. You will have to accept CVs by email and this limits slightly how well the candidates may present themselves. It is getting more popular and for some jobs you may value an easy familiarity with the internet.

The response

Once you have decided on the publication and the frequency, you must decide on how to deal with the response. It is polite to reply to each applicant, particularly those who will not go forward to shortlist. Hence the need, mentioned before, to frame the advertisement to exclude the obviously unsuitable. You do not want several hundred no-hope applicants.

The ideal position now is three or four possible candidates, all of which, on paper, could do the job. If that is not the position, then you will have to retrace your steps. If you have too many good candidates, make a choice of four or so and put the other ones on ice, just in case. It is more likely that there are not enough. At this stage remember that employing a sales person is a major investment. It is best to rethink the whole process at this point rather than take what you have. Look at the response. Did it attract too low a calibre of candidate? Consider a more up-market publication or maybe the salary and benefits are out of line with the market. Inappropriate experience? Take a fresh look at the advertisement. It might need rewriting. Too few responses from a local advertisement? Cast the net wider. It could be that your ideal candidate is not looking in situations vacant. In this case, going to a recruitment consultant may be the best course.

Going fishing, part 2 – pulling them in

The interview

Whatever the debate about whether to use psychometric and other testing methods, you will always need to interview. Because it is such a standard part of recruitment, it has taken much rubbishing because of its limitations. It is easy to forget that the interview will give more information on whether you want to employ the person sitting in front of you than any other method. So, think of the interview as the key and the other techniques as ways to reinforce or check out grey areas. Remember, this is how the customers will hopefully see your potential sales eagle – bright eyed and eager to sell.

It is probable that this will be the first of two interviews. You want to get down to two, or not more than three, candidates. One may look like the preferred candidate but, as you judge them, they will be judging you as well. A good fall-back candidate is necessary.

Preparation

At this stage, you are looking for the basics. A quick reminder of *key characteristics*:

(a) work-rate
(b) self-discipline.

Then the *additional desirables*:

(c) qualifications
(d) experience
(e) track record.

The additional desirables can be read from the CV and discussed in detail. It's the key characteristics that can only be found by probing. It is true that psychometric testing is designed to be useful here but it is the application of work-rate and self-discipline that is important. What you want to know is how the candidate uses personality and skills to get results in the job that you want them to do.

It is important to get the style of the interview right. It may be thought that a tough, stressful style will sort out the weaker candidates leaving the battle-hardened survivors unscathed. This is fine if your industry employs buyers with a well-honed technique in verbal bullying. The majority will be regular guys with much to do apart from seeing sales people. The difficult ones will be well-trained and skilled negotiators with an appropriate buyer's block to counter any closing technique. If the sales person is not performing, then the worst verbal drubbing they will get will come from their manager. Yes, you will need firm, relevant questioning and the determination to cut through woolly answers. You also need to give the candidates space to sell themselves. Or the rope to hang themselves; it works both ways.

Well before the interview, read the CV carefully and make notes. Highlight the points of concern or interest. References or qualifications can be verified later for the shortlisted or preferred candidate. Be sensitive to the issue of sexual, racial or religious bias.

It is wise to have a checklist with the main points you are looking for and a scoring system. If you get a complaint from a failed candidate, a formal assessment system would be helpful to you. Pending or unspent convictions, particularly motoring ones, could be of significance. No wheels: no deals.

Wherever the interview is done, make sure there are no interruptions – basics such as ensuring your mobile phone is switched off and making clear that the room is in use.

Face to face

A suggested format for the first interview could be as follows:

1. Start with introduction and pleasantries.
2. Interviewer states position in company and a short profile of the business.
3. Reason for the vacancy is given and its position in the organisation.
4. Discussion of main points of CV and covering letter.
5. More probing discussion relevant to vacancy.
6. General questioning from both sides.
7. Wrap up.

Remember, you are looking is discard the unsuitable and be left with no more than three likely candidates at this stage so there is no need to be too clever. Lets take each stage in turn.

1 Introduction and pleasantries

Initial impact is important but can be overstated. You are not looking for a leading actor. Smart neutral dress is very suitable. If the candidate visited a customer dressed the same, would it be suitable? The candidate will probably be nervous or at least keen to create a good impression and may overdo it. Nothing wrong with this, in fact – too laid back and you might wonder if your aspirant sales person wants the job. Depending on the time of the day and length of the interview, you may want to offer coffee, tea or water. This allows some pleasantries to be exchanged. Rehearse one or two before the meeting. You at least will need to appear to be relaxed and calm.

2 Interviewer states position in company and a short profile of the business

You may be recruiting for a position reporting to yourself. Possibly you are doing the initial screening for someone else. Unless you are recruiting for a household name company, a short description of the business is useful. However, this is an opportunity to check if the candidate has done any research or gone to your website if you have one.

3 Reason for vacancy, brief description and position in the organisation

The advertisement will only have given an outline of the job. To ensure that there is no ambiguity or misunderstanding, it is best to be very accurate about the position. Have a job description prepared and let the candidate have it. If you mis-sell the job at this stage it could lead to worse problems later.

4 Discussion of main parts of CV and covering letter

This is the main part of the interview. The object is to find skills and attitude transferable to the job you want to fill. There is the issue of whether the CV is true and accurate. That is best left to later. You are looking for work-rate and self-discipline as essentials. Initiative and other skills should come out of the right questions.

So how to do it? This is not an exact science and you are relying on some honesty from the candidate. Given the room for invention on both sides, some kind of formal structure is needed. Consider breaking the CV up into progress points, job moves or promotions within jobs. At each stage question the specific success (or failure) of the job, the motivation for moving on and who initiated the change. You are looking for the energy to make things happen.

It is easy to be seduced by a sales person full of enthusiasm for a particular market or product. They will express how keen they are to work with customers to solve problems and evolve solutions. All very laudable and customer satisfaction promises to be high. However, come back down to earth and remember that the person in front of you is paid to bring in orders, as large and clean as possible. A track record of delivering this core part of the job is essential from a supposedly experienced and successful sales person. If your candidate is more proud of solving customer problems than getting customer orders, then you do not have a career sales person. You have a career something else and that is not what you are recruiting for.

This is where you need a checklist. Write down the skills and attributes you are looking for and score them from 1 to 10 or 1 to 5. The following are suggested.

Attributes

- **Capable of describing specific results.** Is your candidate task- or results-oriented? Is there a specific track record of achieving targets with some evidence?

- **Initiative.** You want problem solvers and those who pick up the ball and run with it.

- **Intellect.** Not an easy one to define but if it is painful to watch the candidate, think then it is low.

- **Self-improvement.** Is the candidate self-critical and wishing to do better?

- **Articulate.** Persuasive rather then glib. Quality of thought rather than quantity. Can show up how well prepared is the candidate.

- **Confident.** Or self-assured depending on how you see the job. Not to be confused with pedantic or brash.

Skills

- **Experience in markets, training courses and qualifications.**
- **Computer literate.** You do not need a systems analyst but the ability to report and communicate by computer is essential.
- **Written communications.** Poor spelling is just sloppy. You need clear, unambiguous sentences which make a point. This is a good reason to ask for a CV and covering letter.
- **Driving record.** Hiring someone that already has ten points on the licence is asking for trouble.

5 More probing discussion relevant to vacancy

At this point you should have a good picture of the strengths and skills of the candidate. Now is the time to apply them to the new job. Just as the CV was divided into sections or progress points, the job description can be broken down the same way. For each section you will have questions relating to how the candidate would tackle situations and develop their business. While the questioning over the CV would be specific, here it would be more open allowing the candidate to show initiative, enthusiasm, and industry or product knowledge. In many ways this part is similar to the sales person in front of a customer, the main difference is that the product is the person.

Does the candidate use the time effectively? Is the candidate articulate and precise or woolly? Is it obvious that research has been done? Does the candidate dry up or smoothly pass the questioning back to you when appropriate. There are a variety of questions that can be used to draw out the candidate. Prepare them before the interview and construct them so as to allow good candidates to put forward a persuasive case for their employment. Note any attempts at a trial close on you. How subtly or appropriately this is done is relevant to the type of sales person you want. Are you being drawn into employing the candidate or is your back up against a wall?

General questioning

Here you can include all the motherhood questions about where the candidate would like to be in a few years time and so on. The answers should be well rehearsed from a good candidate and can be part of the winding down of the interview. Personal questions can be asked but be careful. Any suggestion of sexual, religious or racial bias, even unintended, could cloud the outcome of the process. Asking about non-work or social activities in a very open way is useful to see how well rounded is the candidate.

Wrap up

Finish by giving timescales and the next part of the process. If you have ten candidates to interview and intend to shortlist two within the week, then say this. If you offer to contact the candidate, successful or not, by a certain time, then ensure that you will. The candidate may have taken time off work or travelled some way for the interview. Thank them properly. If you do not treat them well then, later, if you want to see them again, they may not want to see you.

Analysing the results

You may have seen several candidates and by the last one, the details of each will be a blur. But, you have been diligently taking notes and scoring under appropriate headings so some analysis can be done. Simply adding up the totals is not good enough. A very low score in a vital area should rule out a candidate even if the overall score is good. Hopefully, the end result is at least two candidates who meet the basic criteria and are worth seeing again. If no one is suitable, then it is back to the drawing board. Just re-advertising may be throwing good money after bad. Go back to the beginning and check where you may have gone wrong. The recruitment companies will offer lots of candidates. Look at their terms and conditions very carefully.

The second and maybe final interview

This is where it gets serious. You may have two or three candidates that can do the job. One may be the favourite but the other two are insurance in case the first pulls out. It is even possible that there are two very different candidates that would do the job in different ways. The second interview is designed to differentiate between them.

It helps to go back to the start and understand clearly what you want and the abilities you are looking for. Once that is done you can plan the second interview. If it seems laborious, remember, your new sales person can cost you a fortune rather than make one if you get it wrong.

You may be looking for a new business sales person to blaze a trail, perhaps someone to strengthen an existing team, or experience of a new market to allow you to expand the business. The second interview should now concentrate on what you want the new person to do. There are basically two approaches; a more rigorous face to face or change the format. The face to face should include a second or third person interviewing. Before the interview, discuss what you are looking for and divide up the tasks. This format gives the non-speaking interviewer observation and thinking time. The alternative is to change the format from interview to presentation. The candidate could be asked to present on a subject or in a way that replicates a sales situation. This will test many of the skills you are looking for in a relevant way.

Whatever you do, just make sure you know in advance what you are looking for. If it is knowledge of a new industry, do some homework on that industry. If it is an ability to put across new concepts, ask for a presentation that tests clarity of thought and communication. Do not do this by yourself. At this stage another opinion is vital.

At the interview, take notes and use a common score sheet. Allow plenty of time. You might need to break the interview at some stage and have a private conference. Be honest with answers to the candidate about the job and company. That does not mean warts and all but it does mean not giving an understanding that could cause trouble latter. Think before you flatter.

Before the offer

The interviews have ended and you have a preferred candidate. You may have a psychometric test result that looks satisfactory. Now, is the CV true and accurate? Are the references sound? The minimum that a reference can offer is confirmation from an employer that the candidate was employed with dates, position and reason for leaving. Obviously the last point may not be applicable with a present employer. Any employer that gives more is asking for trouble. Too many employers have ended up in court after giving references that the employee disagreed with. Hence, a reference is of limited value. Checking the bare facts on the CV can be useful if it is important. If you are looking for a sales manager and the CV states relevant experience, but a check reveals that the candidate was never responsible for staff, then this is crucial.

Hopefully you get to the stage where the candidate is given the thumbs up on all counts. Time for the offer. A few bits of advice. State clearly a probationary period. You will only know if the new sales person is any good when you work with him or her. It is tempting to offer a better salary than others to get someone good into the team. People talk. At some point, it will be known what the new person is earning. Unless you can justify the pay it is best not to do it or, if you have to do it, consider revising all salaries if you are not competitive. At least with those sales people doing comparable jobs and who deserve it.

Send the offer. If it is accepted, then congratulations, more orders are due to fly in the door. If not, well, back two steps and start again.

When it all goes wrong

The opposite of hire is fire. While hiring is an expression of hope and expectation, firing is only failure. You will only know if you have recruited the right person when some time has elapsed and the new hire has shown his or her true colours in attitude and performance. Unfortunately there is little real solution to people who lie on the CV or during the interview. You can check specific details and get the references for what they are worth but you are left with judging what is in front of you. Even if the candidate did not lie, could you have detected the drug user or that person who was about to divorce and would turn to drink?

This is not the book for employment law. Here the issue being tackled is around the business reasons for needing to dismiss sales staff. Failure is not just about not getting orders. It could be customer satisfaction, inability to work with others, failure to engage properly with the set tasks and market and many others. You will need to be very specific over why you are dissatisfied and collect the evidence. You should also have recognised the problem and discussed it with the new hire. A programme of remedial actions should have been agreed and given time to take effect. However, it is assumed that this has been done and not been successful.

Did you recruit the wrong type of sales person? You may have wanted an emphasis on new business but the sales person is only comfortable with contacts that are well known. Perhaps you wanted good technical skills and recruited someone who could not cope with the pressure of making the target each month. You may be able to change the nature of the job or make a move to another department. More common is that the new hire interviewed well but never engaged properly with the job. If the fundamental problem is a complete lack of a vital skill, such as work-rate, there is no point in going any further. It could be a company culture problem. You may want self-supporting and self-motivated staff but your poor performer needs constant management and reassurance. If the result of hiring the wrong person is that friction will never go away, then bite the bullet and put on the black hat.

More difficult is dealing with sales staff who have been with the company for some time. Selling is a complex and high-pressure career. Success and failure are easy to measure and can be very public. Even the best can weary of it or become complacent. Keeping your team motivated and full of energy all the time is almost impossible. Everyone will have a bad patch at some point. Difficulties at home come to the desk and few staff wish to discuss such issues with their manager. Spotting the sales person who is burned out or who has lost interest is difficult. Some of the indicators are when work-rate goes down, customer contact suffers, and more time is spent in the office. This is not necessarily a matter of deciding when to fire but how to resolve the difficulty before it gets ugly. Consider a change of role or similar to refresh the person. If it is going to be terminal then come to a satisfactory agreement on the best way out. To have an unfair dismissal case or a nervous breakdown on your hands will soak up management time and everyone is a loser.

No mention yet of those supposedly typical sales person misdemeanours, fiddling expenses and watching telly at home instead of being on the road. You should have an expenses policy with guidelines and appropriate costs. While some flexibility is good, gross abuse is simple fraud and is dealt with in the same way as any other serious breach of discipline. As for the sales person at home watching television, look around the office. Who is staring out of the window, surfing the internet, chatting at the coffee machine. How sales people use their time is up to them. What they achieve is important. If the sales forecast, reports, expenses and orders do not build a picture of someone on top of the job, then that is when a serious appraisal is justified.

There are more serious but subtle breaches of contract that are far more difficult to spot. Is your sales person doing a bit of moonlighting and selling something else with no connection to your business? In a highly commissioned environment, is there some secret bribery going on? Those are the sorts of things that could keep you awake at night rather than if a sales person claimed a few extra car miles.

Whatever the reason for concern over the performance or discipline of a sales person, get evidence and legal advice, and make time to air the situation in a non-threatening environment. It could be that you have got it wrong or, in the background, is a difficult personal crisis which does not need your making it worse.

7

Making the Team

It all seems so simple. You have something to sell so you get some sales people. Once they are on board, you worry about difficult things such as design and production. All that needs to be decided is whether they sell from a desk or you get them a car. That's about it, then? The answer is no. There are many types of sales people and different selling roles. When you make your team, you will get different skills and ambitions. Get it wrong and you lose your hot selling machine before you can say forecast. Alternatively you could be saddled with people who cannot deliver your business plan and you have a dilemma over what to do about them.

Most companies will not be starting from scratch or be able to create a new sales team. Some selling, or attempt at selling will have happened. A fresh look at the sales function is often prompted by specific problems or general unease. One common problem is when the team is stale or not able to respond to market changes or opportunities. The result is low growth and erosion of market share. Another is the problem faced by new companies. The selling may have been done by the founders or by the reaction of an ad-hoc collection of whoever was available. This chapter is designed so you can stand back and take stock of the selling capability you have now and how you can develop it and fine-tune it for high performance. This chapter is split into four sections.

- First, know your business …
- … then create your team.
- Work out what they have to achieve and …
- … how to do it in practice.

First though, a quick overview.

There is a hierarchy of sales roles and many organisations will have a sales team made up of people with a range of abilities. Here is a short table of sales roles with the most complex (and expensive) at the top. The titles are for illustration rather than being definitive.

1 **Global Account Manager.** Deals at board level of multi-national companies. Negotiates frameworks, agreements and policy for supply across all countries.

2 **National Sales Account Manager.** Capable of managing complex sales to national companies at board level. Also deals with local subsidiaries of multinational companies.

3 **Sales Account Manager.** Manages relationship with a variety of accounts from small to large. Can be complex or high value.

4 **Business Account Manager.** This title used to be applied to a semi-marketing role. It now generally applies to new business selling. Because of this, it spans a range of abilities from mundane to board level.

5 **Sales Representative.** Low to medium complex selling and frequently combined with a high call rate on customers.

6 **Internal Sales Person.** Manages a wide variety of customers by telephone, email, etc. Low to medium complexity. The internal version of the Sales Representative for customers whose business is too low or infrequent for regular visits.

7 **Telesales.** Structured selling for low complexity sales. Can be actively selling out to lists of contacts or passive response to inbound callers.

8 **Sales Assistant.** Usually in retail.

9 **Electronic or Direct Selling.** Use of the internet, catalogue or advertising. Internet selling can allow more complex customer choice then simply description and part number as Dell has shown with computer sales.

The costs of people and transactions decrease as the list goes down. Conversely the cost of marketing goes up. At the top of the list, the sales person goes to the customer, at the bottom, the customer comes to you.

Large sales-oriented companies may employ all of the above in the sales function. Small companies could employ two or three categories. The issue for companies in the SME sector is who to employ and how to ensure they are effective. Getting it wrong can have disastrous results; missed sales, increased selling costs and de-motivated staff. How then can you get the team that matches the business? Only by knowing your business in detail, knowing your customers and knowing where you plan your business to be in the future. Let us look at each in turn.

First, know your business ...

You could do a business analysis that would keep a Harvard MBA employed for some time. Do not bother. It is tempting to think that the big multinationals employ a regiment of Harvard MBAs to define strategy and oversee implementation. Don't be fooled. Multinationals are not always hotbeds of originality, creativity and clear thinking. You will almost certainly be capable of an analysis of your business that could at least match common practice elsewhere.

Though we are not talking rocket science, you do need accurate data on your business. Even if you have a fully computerised system it is surprising how the holes show when you need management data. This book assumes that you have good, accurate data. There was a time when everyone understood with computer systems that garbage in was garbage out. Now we take computers for granted, it can be garbage in, gospel out. If you cannot be sure of counting accurately what you sell and to whom, then simple analysis is impossible, let alone introducing commissions and bonuses that are based on them.

You need to build a profile of the business; margins, order values, number of accounts and so on. This will help to show you where you are now and should guide you to where you should be going. Such analysis should be done anyway as part of your planning and there are many books and consultants to help. For planning the sales function, you need specific information on the nature of orders and customers. As a start look at the following.

1. How many customers? This is important, both the number and how active they are.
2. Rank the customers in order of value of business placed. Do this for two or three years if possible.
3. Find the margin for each order if possible.
4. Assuming you have a product mix, who buys what?

If you cannot get the information above in a reasonably straightforward way, then your systems are not good enough. If you have collected a good amount of information, then you can quickly summarise the basis of the business. It is common to find the 80/20 rule. 80% of the business comes from 20% of the customers. However, 80% of your margin may not come from those customers. Within the 80% of your customers there could lurk those who could be more profitable then the bigger customers. What they buy is important. Do the small customers buy without much effort or do they soak up as much attention as a substantial customer?

At this point you should know the type of business that comes in, from where and where the profit is. Now the customers need to be analysed. You know how many there are and the good and bad in terms of profitability. It could be that you just want more of the same. It is also likely that the information highlighted some unpleasant facts. The result could be that you want a different mix of customers and the profile of the ideal customer is one that you have put little effort into acquiring. Try to answer the following for your customer base.

1. Which customers or groups of customers give profitable business with reasonable effort?
2. Who are the problem customers? Maybe they pay late or do not invest in skills so are always asking for help.
3. Are there customers or markets that are growing where you may have a very appropriate or premium product?

There are more or different questions you could ask depending on the business. The essential point is that you want to home in on where you need to concentrate your efforts.

At this point a SWOT analysis would be a good idea. This is a very old and effective technique to guide your planning. In case the acronym has slipped your mind it stands for:

Strengths
Weaknesses
Opportunities
Threats

To do this effectively, you may need to allow into the discussion people who raise difficult issues and point out that you have no clothes. If you cannot be sure that your organisation can provide this, ask someone from outside who has some knowledge of your business and can comment. This is not a book about business or market planning so if you need to dig more deeply into these techniques, there is no shortage of help on the bookshelves.

All the above looks like a lot of hard work when you have pressing business matters. Just think of it as investment that saves money and aggravation later. It is only now that you can make crucial decisions on the make-up of your sales force. It is not good enough just to work out how to get the business now. You should have a view on where the company needs to be in the future. Only your sales team will bring you there.

Most companies will have a spread in the size of customer and a poorly defined potential market. It is in reconciling the different demands of this reality that vexes most business owners and managers. The answer lies in structuring the team to reflect your market. There are three broad categories of customer that you are likely to have.

1 Those with complex product or buying needs. The complexity can be risk, emotional support, technical, legal and so on. They demand personal attention. This is the realm of the field sales person.

2 Customers who need support and attention. Requirements can be flexible but they may not need or welcome personal attention. Serving these customers can vary from telesales in a call centre environment to skilled desk based sales people.

3 Well defined and often price sensitive products can be sold via the internet, mail order, retail or basic telesales that essentially take orders without selling.

The third category of sales is really marketing so it will not be considered here. It could though be a significant part of your sales and have to fit within your overall sales plan. The first two categories contain a rich diversity of styles and competences. There is plenty of scope for you to promote and develop staff if you want to move your business up the value chain of enterprise.

... then create your team

Time to look at the different types of sales person. If you thought that all sales people were the same, think again. In a previous chapter sales people were analysed and some advice given on recruitment. Those rules and observations hold true for most sales people but there is a wide spread of abilities and aspirations. We will use the definitions given at the start of this chapter.

1 Global Account Manager (GAM)

If you are an SME company you probably do not need this esoteric deal maker. They are the ultimate sales professional, senior enough to have rapport with key figures in giant multinationals but concentrating on the mechanics of selling. They are usually found in multinationals that sell to multinationals. They need to have substantial skills in virtual team management. As well as dealing with their multinational customers, Global Account Managers have to keep the company sales people in different countries on message and selling hard, usually without having direct responsibility for them. If you are an SME, you may pick up a burn-out who can share much experience in return for not spending a lifetime at airports.

2 National Sales Account Manager (NSAM)

If you need to sell complex products at senior levels in organisations, then here is your sales person. They are rarely young and cheap as the partnership selling they specialise in requires some experience and maturity. Managing them is also an exercise in partnership. As they bring great personal skills and market or technical knowledge, then you cannot treat them as minions. You will expect much of them, particularly as you run payroll or sign off their expenses. They will expect much from you in return as their track record is based on working for successful companies that deliver exactly what they promise.

3 Sales Account Manager (SAM)

Here are the bread and butter sales people. They are the mainstay of most field sales teams. They come in all ages, a varying range of abilities, specialities and attitudes. Some drifted into sales and found they preferred it; others made a deliberate move. If they have attended regular training courses, then regard it as a bonus. Be careful here in trying to relate competence with ambition. Some of these sales people will be happy just doing their job with good results for year after year. Many are high performance sales people used to earning good money and see no need to strive for management or change their career. They still expect to be well trained and take their personal development seriously. Quite a few will stay in the same market for many years and simply change their employer. Their list of contacts will be vast and certain customers will be personal friends. The best may not be looking for a job so you may need a head hunter to get the one you want.

4 Business Development Manager (BDM)

The Business Development Manager or BDM has been a hybrid between sales and marketing, often used to start a new product or market before handing over to a sales person or team. It is increasingly being used to describe a *new business* sales person. It is wise to have decided if you really do mean a new business sales person or a marketing specialist. If you want a sales BDM you are looking at a different person from the Sales Account Manager. The two types are often described as hunters and skinners, the BDM gets new customers on board while the Sales Account Manager concentrates on relationships and long-term business. Getting new business is tough, and effective BDMs are rare. You are looking for good impact, discipline, planning and tenacity.

5 Sales Representative (SR)

It is easy to confuse the Sales Representative (SR) with the Sales Account Manager (SAM). SAMs will operate with considerable independence to target accurately for results. They will then use well-honed selling skills to win business. It is common to think you have employed a SAM when in fact you have employed an SR. An SR is in many ways the traditional travelling sales person. The role involves visiting many contacts, mostly existing customers, normally several each day, selling non-complex products. They are an endangered species, squeezed, as they are, between the SAM, who aims to sell high in the target organisation, and low cost telesales and direct mail. The argument for keeping them is that many customers value the personal touch. True enough but, when push comes to shove, the lowest price is often valued highest of all. However, they can excel in some situations. Many have considerable skill in the quick, high pressure sale situation. The model was the Xerox school of photocopier sales person. Focused, determined and with a high work rate, given the right product and concentration of prospects, the sales rep can be formidable. Most sales reps, or at least the better ones, want to move their careers onward at some point.

6 Internal Sales Person

Up to now, the sales people have been field roles. Expensive, usually out of sight but, hopefully, adequately self managed. Internal Sales are at a desk but this does not necessarily mean telesales. Telesales will be dealt with next. While Telesales works within a tightly scripted environment, Internal Sales operate much like field sales but without cars. Many customers do not warrant a visit from a sales person as their business may be too modest or infrequent for such a luxury. Added together, these customers can be a sizable part of revenue so it may be unwise to dump or ignore them. In fact, properly handled, internal selling with focused marketing can serve these customers better then having a sales person drop in for a rare visit. While a field sales person may strive to do 20-25 quality visits per week, an internal sales person can do more in a day. The internal sales person is more likely to send immediately some promised material or do a follow up action. The best internal sales people are just doing an apprenticeship to earn the car keys. This is a recognised route to start a sales career so recruit with that in mind. All the star sales qualities of self discipline, work-rate and empathy with the customer will be demonstrated under your nose; or not, depending on your recruiting skills.

7 Telesales

At this point, selling merges into marketing. As such it is not covered in detail by this book. Telesales can play an important part of your selling effort if you have products or services that fit the model. What is the difference between internal sales and telesales? This can be argued about but I suggest the following.

- Internal sales largely structure their own time and activities while teleselling is tightly disciplined and structured.

- Internal sales have a wide range of selling propositions to suit individual customers. Telesales follow a script and are directed to possible customers.
- Internal sales need product knowledge and broad selling skills. Telesales are not expected to move far from the script and can change products or services with minimal training.
- Internal sales is usually imbedded in the company structure. Telesales is an activity that can be out-sourced.

When should you consider telesales? If the selling proposition is simple and your target market and contacts are precisely defined, then telesales offer a low cost of sale. One advantage of telesales is that you can get a specialist call centre company do a trial campaign. You can then decide if it is an effective selling model.

8 Sales Assistant

We are largely in the world of marketing now. The sales assistant, usually in retail, is at the end of a lot of money spent on advertising and image for commodity products. Though more than just someone to take your credit card (as anyone who fights off a pitch for the extended warranty on a washing machine will know) this sales role is well outside the scope of a book aimed at complex selling environments.

9 Electronic or direct selling

Once a product becomes definable and price sensitive, then the internet opens up as a selling channel. Who would have thought that computers would be sold over the internet? What about electronic auctions? You may have a complex product but spares and consumables for that product could be sold from your internet site. Does your product or service have to be tailored? Put the tools and ordering flowcharts on the site as well. Quite often customers want to do some of the work themselves before calling the sales person.

A general point about the people in these roles. Most sales people fit into three types in terms of teamwork.

- The first is the **individual contributor**. Many sales people just like to get on with their job with as little interference as possible. They may demand resources but, basically, they close the business on their own. While they may be very good at selling, becoming a sales manager or similar advance is unlikely.

- The second type is the **team player**. They prefer being part of a team and supportive peer group. Do not make this type work remotely from home. They get on with their own job but like to rub shoulders regularly to feel they belong.

- Lastly is the **team leader**. The team leader is adept at building a virtual team to win deals. You will recognise the type as you find you are drawn in to do a specific job in a complex sale. They can be management material but it does not necessarily follow. Their ability to use colleagues and then discard them is not a long-term management strategy.

All of these types are useful and a sales force blended from them would be formidable. Only if you gave them appropriate roles though; mix them wrongly and you have a dysfunctional mess.

Finally, work out what they have to achieve

This is the tough one. You want a sales team big enough to capture your market but not waste money on too big a team. Too small and business will slip through your fingers. Also, the targets should stretch the team but not demoralise them. Make it too easy though and the team will be complacent and not use their skills. It sounds like an impossible task to reconcile these conflicts. In some ways it is; in fact it is unlikely that you will ever get it just right all of the time. Management is not about getting to the point when you can switch on autopilot. As you develop both the market and individual sales people, you will continually monitor and adjust. To do this you need to understand your market and your strategy.

There are four considerations in planning how to structure the sales team and allocate their duties:

- the geographic territory
- the market or markets
- the product or service you sell
- who you sell to.

You have already done some analysis of the customers so you can quickly focus on the main considerations which will influence the structure. Let us look at the above in more detail.

The geographic territory

Here, the sales force is divided up by areas of the country. It has been the traditional way to cover the market or markets by a field based selling team. Sales people covering areas some distance from the office would be home based. If you have a single or simple market, then this is the best structure. It is tempting to create local offices for sales and service in the centre of the main local areas. A company based in the south may open an office in the north; and the other way round as well. Think this one through. If it does not add business value then forget it. A local sales office needs the same disciplines as the main office. If well led, it can provide a welcome focal point for staff who may feel isolated if purely home based.

Divide by market

Whether to divide by market, geography or product has been a preoccupation of sales management for some time. Division by market has been driven by the perception that when a sales person is dedicated to a market or a single large corporation, then that market knowledge is of value to the customer. This can be true with some industries requiring very specialist knowledge to understand the opportunities and apply solutions. The disadvantage is that it is an inefficient way to cover geographic territory. Large companies can create a team to cover a market and then divide them into geographic areas. The problem is for small companies who may have one specialist sales person to cover a whole country. You need to consider very carefully whether market knowledge is so important to your selling effort that organisation by market is more important than by geographic area. Remember, some customers will not like the reality of your sales people also talking to their competitors in order to cover the market. Will they be as open as you would like?

Product specialists

Do you provide a range of complex products? If so you may consider having sales people or teams specialising in part of the range. This has been popular in the IT and telecoms industry where it was felt that the copious product knowledge of the sales team would ensure that a competitor could not outsell with a better barrage of facts. It is true that many products are becoming more complex in their capabilities while it is intended that they should be easier to use. Selling these capabilities without sounding bewildering is no mean task. The product specialist is more use when dealing with an equally knowledgeable customer. When planning to use product specialists, it is useful to remember that they are still sales staff. You can acquire a closet techie who forgets that closing the deal is what counts.

It is possible to employ all of the above in one company. The large computer multinationals were/are paranoid about being outsold and used every structure in a complex management matrix. A significant customer could have three sales people from the same company trying to call and sell. What's more, they were often in competition with each other. Add to this the use of resellers to promote the same products and you can see the confused result. If you have a rule that says only the successful sales person gets the commission, then you have a sales force at each other's throats. You can keep the peace by paying commission to all those who contributed to the sale. This means that your cost of sales goes up. The worst case is if all sales people achieve their targets and commissions and the company overall falls short. If your company is smaller, you may not think this applies to you. However, just broaden your selling effort to include telesales or internet and conflicts will start.

Who do you sell to

If you want your sales people to see customers, then the customers need to want to see the sales person. Getting the first appointment is difficult; repeating that appointment to build a relationship needs more than persistence. It may seem relatively simple; younger, less experienced sales people target middle to lower level customer contacts and grey haired wrinklies lunch the big cheeses. It is more subtle than that. The more junior sales person is valued for availability and energy. The more experienced is valued by customer senior management for the ability to make things happen. Selling can be complex and selling at senior levels requires a blend of more interpersonal skills. When you appoint a sales person to sell high and get the big deals, remember that you will rely on that person's judgement. You will have to make resources available to meet the commitments made by your senior sales person. It is wisdom you want, not age. Hopefully the two go together but you need the sales person's history to bear it out. Don't put someone in that position who has a judgement you do not trust.

Your market may be middle order, over-worked buyers who waste little time on relationships. Here, don't bother with lunch and golf selling. High work-rate, focused closing machines who come to the point with much economy will serve you well.

The point is, work out both whom you sell to now and whom you want to sell to in the future. If you have the right material, you can grow and train your team into new roles or consolidate effectively those who are comfortable where they are.

Setting the targets

If there is one area of sales management where you are guaranteed to get a hard time, it is in setting targets. Of course, you do not need to set targets. If you employ the best staff you can afford, they will do the best possible performance. This is probably wishful thinking but, even if it is not, the best reason for not having sales targets is if you do not have business targets either. If you do have business targets such as profits, revenue, growth or whatever, then the appropriate people have to own their part in contributing to success. You can decide on how rigorous the targets can be but be careful on one matter. Make sure that what you measure can be measured accurately. A later chapter discusses this aspect in more detail; here we want to look at what to measure.

The primary issue is whether there is history or not. If there is history of accounts, revenues or other parameters, then the selling job could be based on getting more of the same. If there is no history then target setting is difficult. Either way, setting targets boils down to just two methods unless you have a lot of time on your hands. You can extrapolate from where you are or analyse to achieve some specific objectives.

Needless to say, extrapolating only works if you have some history. If the business plan calls for 10% more sales, then increase targets by 10%. Sounds crude but this is the normal practice for many companies. If there is a degree of double counting, then the individuals' targets may have to go up 15 or 20% to get the real 10% increase. The main problem here is that over time it is obvious that some sales people have better geographies or accounts then others. Is it luck or hard work? You must judge and adjust if necessary. If it is luck or poor allocation, then you must act. In a commission-based environment, gross unfairness can undermine morale very quickly. That's enough about extrapolation. Time to get complicated.

If there is no history or it is unreliable, different tactics are required. Entering a new market is the normal reason for not having any history though allowing an existing market to be poorly covered gives similar results. Both can be treated as new business situations. Investing in sales effort assumes that the market has potential. Market research can give good information on the size of a market and the number of possible customers. Niche products fitting into niche markets are more difficult to research but some information is always available. The problem is what do you do with the information in terms of setting targets?

If you are entering a new market or building up an existing one, then you should work out the business plan and define targets based on that. Let us look at the steps to building up a market.

- Market research.
- Build market awareness.
- Get early customers.
- Build market share.
- Sustain profitable business.

The targets can change as the market builds and the timescales can be a matter of judgement. Taking each in turn:

Market research	Purely marketing, not sales.
Build market awareness	Mostly marketing. Possible telesales.
Get early customers	Set minimum number of early customers. Fully functional pilot sites. Measure by reference sites which allow PR.
Build market share	Measure revenue. Proportion of customers in market using product.
Sustain profitable business	Measure revenue. Measure margin.

Getting targets right is both an art and a science. You may have to revisit your targeting several times over a year to ensure that what you chose is effective and achievable. It is an essential discipline for a sales team but should not become a battlefield. The targets should add up so as to deliver the business plan. Each of the sales team should know that they own part of that plan.

How to do it in practice

To illustrate all of the above, here is an example. ABC Data Enterprises Ltd (ABCDE Ltd) has developed a software application for the Oil and Gas Industries. Business is tough but has grown with good profits as the product has established a good reputation. The core product is sold as a turnkey system, that is, complete with computer hardware bought in from the manufacturer. There are some additional complementary software products and service is an important source of revenue.

The business plan recognises that continued growth will be difficult unless they develop new markets. The pharmaceutical industry is thought to offer opportunities and a way should be found to enter that market. There may be scope to become a computer hardware reseller. At the moment computer hardware is bought only to run the software developed by ABCDE. However, if more hardware were sold, then there would be a better deal from the computer supplier as well as profit from increased sales. Finally, increasing the range of bought-in and resold complementary software would strengthen the appeal of the core product and increase support revenues.

The sales team consists of three field sales account managers with a sales administrator. They report to the Managing Director as the company is not big enough for a separate sales manager.

This is a classic business situation as a company grows, gets momentum but needs another investment in sales to move beyond a start-up situation. It is essential to protect the existing market for steady revenues while a new market is built up. So how should the team be modified to allow the company to grow?

There are a number of ways to increase selling effort here and the one described follows a cautious policy. With the opportunities in the Oil and Gas Industry moving to consolidation, further selling investment in the core product is unwise. One sales person can be moved to develop the pharmaceutical market. Is this a good move though? Is market knowledge important? The product is complex and training a new sales person would mean a substantial delay. It is decided to move the most experienced sales person to pharmaceuticals. Market research has indicated that less than twenty companies would be potential buyers so the most suitable could be focused on quickly.

To build the new business of computer hardware reselling, a new sales person will be recruited. The ideal candidate will be an up and coming Business Development Manager with computer reselling experience. The Oil and Gas industry would be targeted first using the company reputation in turnkey systems for credibility.

Selling the complementary software, service and computer peripherals requires a high volume of calls. They are well defined products but the existing sales people only had time to sell them when offering the complex core product. It is decided to recruit an internal sales person to concentrate on these simple products. To assist with marketing, a PR and advertising agency has been appointed to provide attractive promotional material and case studies. The website will contain data sheets, prices and customer endorsements.

The above looks straightforward enough. Some simple targeting and the team is ready for action. However, the devil is in the detail. As the targets for each person are set, the difficulty of keeping it simple and avoiding internal wars becomes apparent.

Sales Account Managers for Oil and Gas Industry

Targeted by revenue. Credited with all hardware, software and service contract on first order for turnkey system. Not on subsequent additions or upgrades except for an upgrade to the core application. This is so they focus on gaining new customers for the core application.

Sales Account Manager for Pharmaceutical Industry

Has a target to achieve a reference sale in a major pharmaceutical company within six months. Has a modest revenue target to encourage the winning of two more accounts in the following six months.

Business Development Manager

Has a target based on the total gross margin on the resold

computer hardware. This ensures that the hardware is not sold at a loss. Not credited with hardware sold turnkey which is the responsibility of the Sales Account Managers.

Internal Sales

Targeted on revenue from complementary software and service. A separate target of gross margin on any resold software or computer peripherals. There is a conflict here on computer peripherals with the Business Development Manager. The company wants the customer to use the lowest cost method of sale. The BDM will want to capture this business and could keep quiet about opportunities to stop the Internal Sales getting the credit. The result would be fewer sales. It is decided to credit both the BDM and Internal Sales with peripheral orders to maximise cooperation.

Everyone has an appropriate target which should motivate them to get the kind of business that the company wants. The total targets should add up to the revenue turnover in the business plan. Don't forget to add a bit for the peripherals which could be double credited. The addition of the targets could be 105% of plan so that the real revenue is 100%. This approach will only work if your systems are good enough to correctly credit the sales team with those products they are targeted on without much tiresome manual counting. If you cannot be absolutely sure of your systems or ability to credit do not try any complicated targeting. It would be better to have a team target based on total revenues than something specific but flawed. If you are paying commission or bonuses on results and get the numbers wrong, you are in big trouble.

Targeting of the sales team does not end there. They will have a variety of tasks of value to the company. These are covered in the next chapter, Getting Organised.

8

Getting Organised

This is the planning, structure and administration chapter. It could be boring but it won't be. That is because if you get it wrong, you could be out of a job or have a failed business. It is divided into several sections which are;

1. Setting the ground rules
2. The Sales Agreement
3. Forecasting
4. Reporting
5. Account or territory plan
6. The sales meeting.

This is a substantial chapter but the topics discussed form the glue to bind the team together and deliver your business plan. Don't try to do it all at once but introduce as changes occur and the team sees the value in the new structures.

1 Setting the ground rules

If you want an effective, disciplined sales force you need disciplines that are effective. If you do not, you could have a ship of loose cannons; interesting but a disaster. One of the good reasons for discipline and structure is to do with empowerment. It sounds like a contradiction but you can only allow people to be empowered if they know their job, what is expected of them and, most important, their limits. In this chapter we will look at how to define what you want a sales person to deliver to the company and how the company rewards and encourages the sales person. If you do not have any of these procedures, you are creating trouble for yourself and your sales team. So many staff regard this control and administration as mere bureaucracy. It is not and too many rows and disputes are caused by staff and management not tackling the nuts and bolts of their jobs until a problem surfaces.

In a perfect world, you would have carefully followed this book and now have a team of sales road warriors straining at the leash to get the business. The inside team is poised by the phone and computer screen, ready to shout orders! The website is already counting the hits. You relax before transforming the rest of the company.

Unfortunately the world is not perfect. You team varies from excellent to must do better. A mixture of what you have inherited and what you could afford. This is no different from any other part of the company but, as we have seen, sales has its own particular management problems. It is no use running your sales team like the design department or accounts. It is not that it is more difficult, just different.

There is one very important and fundamental difference that you must not forget. **A sales team is measured by results, not by measuring and controlling every action they do.** This is *rule number one*. It does not mean that you do not give instructions or advice. It does mean that given the right structure, people and support, you assess and measure what your team achieves in orders and market feedback. If you find that you are constantly telling your team how to do their job, then you may have a problem. If you are telling one sales person how to do his or her job, then that person has a problem. This so important that I will repeat it. Worry about and monitor what your team achieves, not how they do it. Sales people are a group of knowledge users who have to be empowered to be effective. The word 'empowered' is so over-used that I hesitate to use it. In this case it is correct and essential. Your team will be out of sight for a lot of the time so invest in training if you have concerns. If you are a control freak, managing a sales team will give you a stressful time. Unless you are running a call centre, the internal sales people will also need space to do their best.

Now, this does not mean that your team is uncontrolled and doing as they like. They will work within a system of expectations, requirements and reports so there is no ambiguity over what is to be delivered. You will help them achieve for success and they will in turn will give you forecasts and sales orders so production and stocking can be planned as accurately as possible. The art is in asking for the minimum necessary to plan the business while, at the same time, tracking the competence and progress of the sales person. It is tempting to measure only what can be measured. It is also tempting to want to measure what is important but cannot be measured. If you pay bonuses or commission, it is vital to get these right. Disputes over meeting targets that pay money can be bitter and corrosive. Getting it right is possible if you recognise and avoid the traps.

When managing the sales team, you want to give them the freedom to act creatively and responsibly. If you are a sales manager, you may be able to devote all your time to this. If you are the business owner, you will have other demands but want to be sure the sales team is adding real value without your constant attention. Empowerment was mentioned but how much power to entrust to individuals with a range of competencies? Rule number one was that you do not measure how your team does the job but what they achieve. It is crucial then to put a lot of thought into what you want from the sales function. Only when you have done this can you give direction to the individual sales people.

A business needs to plan to survive. For cash flow and other reasons, the future level of business, the next month, next quarter and rolling twelve months needs to be predicted and budgeted for. Targets for company growth and profitability should be set. The marketing plan defines product changes, new products, existing and new markets. Investments will be targeted where there is best return. Making this all happen, both gathering market information and delivery of revenues is the responsibility of the sales function. The correct targeting of the sales function has to relate directly to business needs. If this is forgotten then you can either burden the sales people with unnecessary work or omit a crucial deliverable. The important point is to formally relate the work of sales with the business plan. So many companies, large and small, employ sales people and then either not target them correctly or not target them at all but merely see what they bring in.

Providing a targeting and reporting structure is not complex but it is important to get it right. Remember, part of an employee's feeling valued is based on your competence to get rewards and demands right.

There are five main methods to give direction and structure to the sales team.

(1) **The Sales Agreement.** This defines what the sales person delivers and the resulting rewards.
(2) **Forecasting.** This predicts future business and allows the business to plan cash flow, manufacture, stocking and product mix.
(3) **Reporting.** The channel for market information and progress.
(4) **The Account or Territory Plan.** How and where to get the best business.
(5) **The sales meeting.** To communicate and encourage.

The relative importance of these management devices depends on the nature of an individual business. However, the most important and crucial to get right is the sales agreement and that is the one to tackle first.

2 The Sales Agreement

You cannot judge the effectiveness of your sales force on what they achieve without knowing what you expected from them. In the previous chapter on making the team, you worked out the size of the sales function and how to target an individual sales person. The next step is giving all the sales people their own statement of what level of performance is expected and how the company will reward them. You would never recruit machine operators and tell them to find their way to the shop floor and make as many widgets as they felt comfortable with. Yet so many companies do this with sales people. The sales agreement reinforces rule number one, that you set out what you want to happen and use training and resources to ensure that it is done in the best manner.

The sales agreement is not a job description. The job description is done once for a specific role and describes that role in terms of its place in the organisation, reporting structure, and general requirements. The sales agreement is updated at least once a year. It changes as the company evolves and the market moves. If having a sales force is a strategic decision, then the sales agreement is part of the tactics used to make the function relevant and in tune with company needs.

The sales agreement is an important document. It could be central to an employee dispute and have a legal status. Draw it up with care and allow room for manoeuvre. It is there to help you plan the business and for the sales people to know what they are expect to do. Do not allow it to become a cause of contention.

The agreement has four main sections.

- The first defines the overall scope of the job.
- The second adds the essential measures of the job.
- The third gives additional objectives, important to the business.
- The forth sets out commissions and/or bonuses.

The first section is to define the main task of the sales person. Put in here the overall boundaries such as the territory, products sold and so on. The second section is a statement of the main measured targets. This is usually the volume of sales measured in revenue. It can be the gross margin for a reseller or wholesaler. At this point it would be useful to mention *rule number two*. **Do not formally measure that which cannot be accurately measured**. It seems too simple to be stated. Why issue it as a rule? The answer is that it happens all the time and never ceases to cause trouble. Can you accurately record the sales by revenue correctly attributed to an individual sales person? Think about it. You may have a small business and orders and responsibilities clearly defined. However, once the business grows, life gets more complicated. You could have a sales person selling directly to a customer. At the same time you may have a reseller, managed by another sales person, also selling to that customer. This is just one scenario. There are plenty more. Even more fundamentally, is your administration and computer system capable of supplying accurate and timely information? If you cannot measure accurately what you want to measure, a common trap is to get round this difficulty by measuring instead what you *can* accurately measure. If this measure is not relevant, then this will fool no one so it is best avoided.

It may seem obvious but the main revenue figure or margin contribution for each sales agreement should be added together to make the total target revenue or turnover for the company. This can be forgotten as you change and modify the numbers to account for particular people and territories. There may be an element of double counting as well. Just remember that you do not want the team to all make their targets and earn a good bonus while you fail to make the company revenue target.

Counting sales revenue as the main measure of performance is most common. There are other measures that can be used. Signing up new customers, retention of business and so on. It is up to you to decide which is the critical deliverable of the sales function to the business. There could be more than one. For these main, critical, metrics just remember rule number two. If you are not sure if you can measure exactly then work out how you can. It is all part of managing a business.

The next decision is how frequently to measure. This could be weekly, monthly, quarterly or yearly. Are you looking for consistency, month after month? Are orders large and only occur a few times a year? The longer the sales cycle, the more important the reporting and forecasting becomes; these will be discussed later. If it is important to you to predict future business and keep it above a certain level, then you may want to reward for this to be delivered. Remember, this agreement is to deliver back to the business the information and performance it needs so it can be well managed.

At this point, you have defined the key deliverables from the sales function and are satisfied that you can measure them. But, that is not the only role of sales. Your team is the main contact with the market and you may want them to do more than just get business. Not only that, but you may want them to spend time doing things that are good for the business but may be difficult or distracting for a sales person.

You may be lucky and have a team who see their role as encompassing all that a good sales function can do. Unfortunately that is the kind of luck that wins lotteries and so is spread thinly. Sales people will concentrate on the key metric, usually revenue, and do it in the most economical way. Not only that but they will also hunt for low hanging fruit – quick, easy business which may drop anyway. If that's good enough for you, then fine. If not, then the agreement needs to contain objectives that drive the business plans. These objectives take two forms, one to do with selling and the other about reporting.

Take the objectives around selling first. To meet your business or marketing plan, you may want to concentrate on particular markets, geographic areas, social groups or whatever is vital to deliver business growth. If the sales force is the primary way to deliver the plan, then the agreement has to clearly state what is required. Here are a few examples of objectives.

- Obtain signed contract with a new customer each month.
- Establish pilot site for new product before end of current fiscal year.
- Sell maintenance contract with at least 50% of product sales.
- Meet Financial Director of key accounts once each quarter.

These objectives could be important for the long-term growth of the business but do not always have a specific revenue attached to them. They are about growth and quality. If your sales team will do it anyway, you probably do not need this book. Look at your business and marketing plan and check through that your sales team are correctly directed and motivated to deliver on it.

There is an important warning on this process and it is rule number two again. It is tempting to include all sorts of desirable objectives but, unless they can be accurately defined, do not put them in the sales agreement. Take quality for instance. A very desirable objective is to improve the quality of customer contact. Why not put in, 'Improve quality of customer satisfaction'? If you have an annual or quarterly survey of your customers with some measurement of satisfaction, then go ahead. If not, then do not even think about it. Still like to do something? Then measure the number of times an order is changed after it is placed. It is based on the idea that good customer contact and satisfaction is based on the sales person getting it right first time. Simple to do and to measure. But, is it a real measure of customer satisfaction? Are you doing it because is measurable rather than it is relevant? Do not make a rod for your own back. If quality is an issue, tackle it some other way. If, at the end of the year, or other measuring period, you cannot be precise that an objective is satisfied, then do not put it in.

At this stage, you have a main measure and certain objectives that are judged key to developing your business strategy. It is most likely that the period of validity is a complete fiscal year. It can be done every quarter but drawing up a fresh document is time consuming unless your business calls for it. However, events can impact any business for good or ill so allow some room for manoeuvre. Put into the agreement a time for review. Objectives can be found to be not realisable or a major customer can stop buying or go bust. Targets can be set too low. This last one can be tricky. There is a difference between raising a target because the sales person is too successful and setting too low a target for reasons that come to light later. You will have to be open and transparent about the methodology for setting targets. This will help prevent sandbagging (sales people secretly holding back orders until targets have been set), deal with bluebirds (totally unexpected orders that required no effort) and less than honest information from sales people on the potential from accounts.

The last part of the agreement deals with salary and any bonus or commission. Payments should be spelt out in the agreement in a clear and unambiguous manner. Not only what will be paid but when.

Money will be dealt with later as it deserves a chapter to itself.

The agreement should be signed by the sales person and the appropriate level of management. It is a serious document and agreement should mean just that. If the sales person does not sign and the discussions go beyond reasonable dissent, it can be considered a matter of formal discipline.

Time to take a look at a typical sales agreement.

Sales Agreement for John Smith

This agreement to cover Financial Year 2002. Start date 1st April 2002.

Products

All company products except spares.

Territory

The counties of Berkshire, Wiltshire, Hampshire and Dorset.

Revenue

A total revenue for the year of £1.2m. This value to be that of the customer invoice net of VAT, any discounts, packaging and deliver charges. Invoices valid up to close of business on the 31st March 2003.

Quarterly revenue totals must be equal or greater than the following for bonuses to apply.

Q1	£300K
Q2	£200K
Q3	£350K
Q4	£350K

Management Objectives

MO1 At least one new customer should be gained each month. A new customer is one who has not bought any products for at least five years and places an order for a minimum of £10K. This MO is measured by the placing of a clean order by the last working day of the calendar month.

MO2 At least one contact on each customer site should receive a quality survey form twice a year and 80% return a completed form. The list of customer contacts should be completed by the end of the first quarter. The customer survey will include all returns received by the last working day of the third quarter.

MO3 Each quotation should include a service contract and at least 50% result in an order for a minimum of the basic service. This will be measured each quarter.

MO4 A forecast of business to be ready on the first working day of each month.

MO5 A report on the state of business and competition to be completed the end of business of each quarter.

Compensation

Your compensation for the current financial year will be as follows.

Basic salary £30,000.00

On target salary £50,000.00

The commission of £20,000.00 will be paid at a rate of £16.666 per complete £1,000.00 of revenue until 100% of target is achieved. From 100% up to 130%, the rate is doubled to £33.332. The maximum is capped at 130%. Commission is measured monthly and paid on the first month of the following quarter.

For achieving the minimum revenue given above each quarter a bonus of £500 will be given payable with commission.

Bonuses will be paid for achieving Management Objective, as following.

BO1. For MO1, £100 is paid for each new customer up to a maximum of 20 customers in the financial year. To be paid quarterly with commission.

BO2. For MO2, £1000 to be paid at the end of the financial year with any final commission.

BO3. For MO3, £500 will be paid each quarter with commission for that quarter.

BO4. There is no bonus attached to MO4. It will be taken into account for any increase in basic salary.

BO5. There is no bonus attached to MO5. It will be taken into account for any increase in basic salary.

Signed for company........................

Signed by sales person.....................

The above agreement is simple, unambiguous, with all metrics capable of measurement, and payment terms precise. It should accurately reflect the needs of the business. Ideally it should stretch the sales person so that making the bonuses needs going that bit further. Too stretching and it can be de-motivating. Variants of the above can be used for most sales positions, internal, on the road and telesales. While it uses rule number one, it incorporates sufficient feedback to monitor progress and highlight problems or reward over-performance.

The next step after the sales agreement is to work out a sales plan with the sales person. This is to plan how the sales person will achieve the agreement. Most of this involves the account or territory plan and they will be discussed at the end of this chapter.

3 Forecasting

Managers and business owners need to plan matters such as cash flow and production. So, they ask sales people for a forecast of orders expected over a future period of time, a week, a month, quarter or year. This is a very reasonable request, in line with business needs but it leads to no end of resentment and frustration for all concerned. Lack of accurate information means bad planning and a bank or shareholders may question the competence of a business owner or director if results are not in line with predictions. For the sales person, it means administration, paperwork and bureaucracy. Worse, for the sales person, it may result in being asked questions to which there may be no ready answer.

Why can the business forecast meeting be so fraught? Some sales people are just so much on top of their job that predicting orders is done with confident precision. If your team fits this description, then pass over the next section. Most teams though have a wide variety of abilities and even the most competent people can find forecasting difficult. Add to this a business owner, not a specialist in sales, trying to run sales as well as everything else and tension can mount. Ask a definite commitment from a sales person, which depends on vague customer information, and you have a person who is very vulnerable. Even with good sales people it can be very difficult to predict accurately when an order is due. Events outside the control of the sales person can completely change the situation. Despite this, a manager can get increasingly heavy in demanding when an order will come in. When an order slips back without an adequate reason, the competence of the sales person is then discussed. A sales person may give copious information on all the good work being done to generate business and show incredible ability and worth to the company. But, ask for the exact moment some of this activity will result in a large, clean order and information becomes more slippery.

How is it possible to cut to the facts and get an accurate picture of business? It can be the case that the problem lies in the manager asking the wrong, or perhaps not relevant, questions of the sales person and the sales person not asking the customer the right questions. Information is key but information on its own is not knowledge or wisdom. The information needed is that which establishes the customer buying cycle. From this, the sales person can plan the selling cycle. Once this is done, forecasting becomes logical rather than guesswork and the whole business starts to make sense.

These cycles will be looked at in some detail in the next chapter. They are not only important to the forecasting process but underpin the discipline of the sales person. This book is not about dealing with irrational impulse buying. Serious buying and selling go through fairly predictable and logical steps even if the buyer and the sales person may not be conscious of it. It is true of most industries and products and whether the selling is quick or lengthy. Armed now with knowledge of the buying cycle, the manager can work through the selling cycle with the sales person. A possible date that the business arrives can be mutually agreed and planning begins.

As the detail of the selling cycle will be dealt with in the next chapter, here we will deal with the mechanics of the forecasting process. At its most basic, you want to know what orders or revenue will arrive over a period of time to a varying degree of certainty. The various stages of the selling cycle could be, depending on industry, some or all of the following.

(1) Identify interest
(2) Influence outcome
(3) Qualify opportunity
(4) Assess the competition and submit proposal
(5) Discuss the proposal
(6) Close the deal.

You can give different titles to the above or ask more detailed questions. The pattern though remains the same, just your need for more specific information varies. Each stage has a number and at each stage the sales person needs to confirm timescales with the prospect. How well the sale is progressing is a subtly different matter from forecasting. In forecasting you want to know, given an effective sales campaign, when the business will arrive and how much will it be worth in revenue, margin or whatever.

An assessment of whether your sales person will ultimately win or not should be separate. Why is this? It is tempting to place a percentage against each of the stages above to show progress. It is even more tempting to add up all the business, factor in the percentage and hence, the total forecast business. This may work if the volume of projects is such that this kind of statistical approach is valid. Mostly, the volume is smaller and the trouble with orders is that you win or lose with no prize for being second. When an outcome is so binary, it is more sensible to judge which will be won and which will be lost. The forecast is then based on adding the wins. Percentages can be useful to more finely tune the forecast; just do not overdo it.

What you want is a simple table of potential business, how much and when. You can do it as a spreadsheet or build it into your sales contact system if that is possible. The headings could be as follows.

Company	Project	Product	Value	Stage	Order

Company (or prospect) Self explanatory, though you may need to sub-divide into subsidiary or location.

Project A large account may have many projects running.

Product If you use the forecast to plan production, this may need to be expanded. The same principal applies for a service relying on availability of people.

Value Total project value. If it arrives in stages, then multiple entries may be necessary.

Stage Where the sale is in the selling cycle.

Order When the order will arrive. It can be more valid to log when delivery is required, hence when you can invoice.

The above is a very simple forecast sheet. You could add columns to cover more detail but, only if it is necessary. Think of it this way, will asking the information, and delaying the sales person, materially affect the business? The bottom line is that you need to know What, How Much and When.

4 Reporting

Your sales force is the eyes and ears of the company. They pick up the opinion of the customer on your products, learn about the competition and seek out new opportunities. They will be the main source of this type of vital information so you need to capture it as efficiently as possible. The trouble is, no sales person likes to spend time recording visits or meetings. Also, you do not want them to be writing reports when they should be selling. For these reasons, think carefully about how much information you want from them on a regular basis.

For the minimum you need from the individuals in the team, consider the most common sales problem. A sales person resigns and admits going to the competition. You have no choice but to suspend the sales person from active work and cut connections to the office systems, email and access to other sensitive data. The normal de-brief is meaningless as full information may not be given. How then to keep up the momentum with active customers and stop them being poached? You stand a chance if the forecasting system is up to date and the basic reporting system has been used. Forecasting has been covered and it can be complex. Reporting can be as simple or complex as you require.

It is essential that you use some form of computerised sales contact system. There are plenty on the market and most can deal with internal and on the road sales staff. The road warriors armed with laptop computers can upload and download data as often as required. The various fields cover customer details, action or to-do lists, diary and so on. These systems are only of use if they are kept up to date. The **customer details**, in particular, are vital to keep correct. The data can be used for customer mail shots and surveys.

What then should be the minimum information recorded by the sales person? I would suggest the following, though your business may be different.

- Current project or projects. This is probably covered by forecasting.
- Last person seen, date, project discussed and outstanding action.
- Next planned visit, contact or action be taken sales person.

The above should be recorded in the notes, reporting or action section of the reporting system. It should be done after each meeting, phone call, letter or other commitment point in the customer relationship. This should be insisted on as a normal professional duty. If a key member of the sales team goes on holiday, is ill or otherwise unavailable, then you can keep on top of the business without looking incompetent in the eyes of your customers. Many sales people, including those who have worked for major sales-driven companies, have not used these disciplines. If they protest at the imposition of such a system, do not back down. Even the biggest and grandest organisations sometimes do not get the basics right.

There is a whole lot more you need to know about your customers. More importantly, it is information your sales staff need to know. However, most of this fits into Account Planning, not reporting, and this will be tackled later.

The second part of reporting is **market information**. The sales force is your main contact with the customer. The customer is the final arbitrator of the quality and relevance of your offering. Unlike you, they talk to the competition and use this to put your sales team under pressure. Customers are not always right, unbiased or fair. They will sometimes lie or mislead. They may, on the other hand, praise your products and loyally buy even though they could get a better deal elsewhere. Your team will have to make sense of this without portable hidden lie detectors. It is not easy even for the most seasoned sales person but it is vital information which needs to be collected and analysed with some discernment.

How you do this varies from one company to another. Putting it into the notes in a reporting system is probably not the best way. If there are very many customers, you will spend too much time sifting through the information. Much of the value here is in spotting trends, useful for both you and the sales force. You can try the monthly written report or verbal at the sales meeting. More about sales meetings later but the choice is one of style and culture of the organisation. Either way, you need to know what you want and have it prepared by each member of the team. Do not over do this. There is only so much information you can usefully use anyway. The following is a start which you add to or drop as you see fit.

- Orders won and why
- Orders lost, why and to whom
- Major competition
- Common objections
- Where we need to do better
- What we do right

This will capture issues about your offering and organisation. It will soon be obvious that your sales team will differ wildly about most of the points except orders won and lost. Here, most orders will be won by the brilliance of the sales person and only lost by an underhand competitor. Interpreting the information is a skill that requires as much knowledge of the sales person as that of the customer. It will uncover trends and issues that can be investigated and addressed. This kind of reporting, taken seriously, is an additional channel for the sales team to let off steam on the matters that affect them. Do not collect data for your own private interest. Show that it matters and that real issues get real action. Some things though are impossible to solve; it saves later heartache to be upfront about that as well.

A word of caution about reporting. Some sales people are very secretive about their account or market knowledge. It is a source of power used when negotiating targets or to be taken with the sales person if they leave for another company. The opposite is also true. Some sales people will dump any amount of data, complaints, information, whinges and opinion on you. Be very clear on what you want, no more or less. Show you use it constructively and that decisions that affect people are based on information they give to you.

5 Account or territory plan

At this point, your sales team should know what they have to achieve, how they will be rewarded, when the business will come in and how to tell you what they have done. The only thing missing is planning how to do it. It is depressing how many sales people are hired and then told to get some business in without any sort of plan of campaign. It is tempting, if you are a business owner and not experienced in sales, just to hire a sales person and think that as you now have an expert you can concentrate on other matters. You may be lucky enough to get an expert who does all the right things. When you ask for the plan, you get a plan. Consistently successful sales people plan and act in a methodical manner. They collect the information they need to be effective where there are opportunities and do not waste much time elsewhere.

These plans are not just for the benefit of the sales person. You need to set targets and offer bonuses and, perhaps, commission. What do you base these rewards on? Building plans with your team should be real partnership. You will be able to apply the business strategy and the sales team will know what is expected of them.

There are broadly two categories of plan, territory and account, and two starting points, new business and ongoing business. To start this in the simplest way, we will look at the account plan for an established customer.

The Account Plan

You have a solid customer, The Widget Company, who place a regular order each month. The expenses for the sales person show that every two months or so the buyer is taken to lunch. At sales meetings, the sales person, Jim, says that the customer is very satisfied and pencils in a forecast amount of revenue for the next six months. All very satisfactory; if only all customers were the same. Then, one month, the expected order does not arrive. You contact Jim who promises to investigate. A little while later Jim calls back. He is puzzled; the call to the Widget Company was strange. The buyer was not available and the assistant could or would not help. You tell Jim to keep on top of it as there is now a hole in the month's orders. Jim is at his desk the next day so you ask him about the missing Widget order. Yes, he tried the buyer's mobile and e-mailed him but no reply. The assistant has not come back either. So you tell Jim to call someone else. How about the buyer's boss? Jim looks sheepish, he admits that he has never met the buyer's boss. In that case, who is he going to call? Jim looks very uncomfortable now. He admits that he is not on casual call terms with anyone other than the buyer and the assistant. He has tried to call names on the organisation chart but gets fobbed off.

Poor Jim. He had a regular earner of an account and thought it was going to last forever. He was completely complacent due to the drip, drip of a regular monthly order and a friendly buyer. He had heard that a new Managing Director had been appointed but that was too distant from his normal contacts. Therefore, Jim had no reason to know that the new MD appointed consultants to investigate some problem areas including the buying department. Jim's buyer took the option offered to accept the lump sum compensation and go immediately. The assistant knew that some suppliers would be investigated, so, best to lie low and stop all orders that were not approved as squeaky clean. Jim only found this out much later, after considerable business was lost and his sales manager gave him a drubbing he would never forget.

Do you have any Jims, just taking the orders, unaware if they are getting as much business as possible or, even, about to get kicked out of the account? If you have a sales strategy of field sales people concentrating on key accounts, then this issue is not one to be tackled when you have more time.

How much time and effort you ask your team to put into account plans depends on your business, the number of accounts and the complexity of accounts. You can send your team on training courses which will do account planning in copious detail. Here though, we will deal with the basics and the basics will cope with a high proportion of the need. The basic needs are to maintain a constant stream of business from an account and to increase it to the maximum available. Your sales team cannot be sure of either unless they have a reasonable level of information. What is reasonable then? That is for you to decide but, to help, let us look at a basic account plan and go through the statements and questions.

Account Plan

Name of company ______________________

Address ______________________

____

____

____

Postcode ______________

Telephone ______________________

FAX ______________________

Website ______________________

Location of other sites. ______________________

____

____

____

____

Nature of Business ______________________

____

____

Turnover ______________________

Why a Key Account? ______________________

____

____

____

____

Location		____________________	
Contacts	Director level	____________________	Met?____
		____________________	Met?____
	Management level	____________________	Met?____
		____________________	Met?____
	Technical level	____________________	Met?____
		____________________	Met?____

Revenue in 2003/2004 ____________________

Revenue in current year ____________________

Potential revenue in current year. ____________________

Potential revenue in 2005/2006 ____________________

Projects ____________________

____

____

____

____

____

____

Competition ____________________

Level of business ____________________

Competition ____________________

Level of business ____________________

The first part – addresses and contact details – seems straightforward. However, many organisations have several locations and knowing the importance of these other locations is vital. If power and influence is concentrated at headquarters, then most of the effort spent in another location will probably be wasted. This has a bearing on any territory plan you draw up. If you allocate by geography then one sales person could have a company headquarters and another sales person one or more further locations. Try not to build in conflict. Understand the account dynamics and give your sales people appropriate ownership.

The section for Nature of Business and Why a Key Account go together. If the account is a baker and you make temperature sensors then it is important to know that you are dealing with a substantial manufacturer. A turnover figure is requested but this may not be the only essential fact about the account. If you have a profile of the ideal customer you may have other key determinants. The Why a Key Account section does require some thought. If it is already a substantial customer, then fair enough. Beware though of sinking resources into accounts that will give you business anyway. If it is new, then rational thought and facts should back up the inclusion. These may be listed later, but, if not, just ask for and document the evidence.

The next section requires work and, usually, highlights the yawning gaps in account knowledge. To know what is going on in an account plus any future plans depends on contacts. The better the quality of contact, the better the quality of information. The more contacts there are, the more checking of facts is possible. If a contact moves on or goes ill then your account knowledge does not stop. Consider carefully the type of contacts you require. If it is not absolutely necessary to cultivate the Managing Director, then do not spend time and effort trying to make it happen. There is a lot of sales work around identifying the correct contacts in accounts. The decision makers and key influencers are not always obvious, as real authority may not follow the organisation chart. Sales training in this area is useful if your sales campaigns are complex.

The section on revenues is simple enough if you have systems that collect information and compile suitable reports. It is often at this point that you find the limitations of your financial data. For instance, the same account has more than one name; the report you want cannot be done on data more than 12 months old, and so on. In the potential business section, this can be actual projects that are progressing and those which are still being kicked around.

Data on competition can be more difficult to obtain and quantify. The customer may consider it sensitive and be reluctant to give too many details. It is unlikely that you would want your dealings to be discussed with a competitor either. Customers may give misleading information on competitors as a bargaining ploy. Asking several people the same question can get closer to the truth. As in most situations, if you don't ask, you don't find out.

If you have a sales team who can fill in an account plan adequately for each of their key accounts then you are very fortunate. It is more normal to find significant gaps. In fact it is only when a sales person tries to fill in an account plan that the true paucity of account knowledge is known. Too few contacts, little account knowledge and so poor forecasting of orders, no idea of what business the competition is taking. You thought it was a safe account, now you see how vulnerable your sales person is.

Your role is to make your staff successful. Helping them plan effectively is one of the most important tasks you will engage in. If a sales person is seeing regular orders from an account, it often takes some persuasion that more work is needed. It will be argued that the effort is better spent in accounts where there is potential but less current business. Resist this argument wherever possible. If current accounts are skimmed lightly, then so will future accounts. Account management is about digging deep and making the most of opportunities. Do not have a team full of Jims.

Once the plan has been filled in, fully or partly, there needs to be action. A sample action sheet has not been shown as it will vary so much for different circumstances. At least some of the action will be around completing the plan. Following that, assuming the potential justifies the effort, then a sales strategy and the resulting tactics will need to be agreed. Sales strategies and tactics will not be discussed here but your role will be to ensure that whatever is agreed is carried out. Unfortunately, account plans are often written only to gather dust from the day after the planning workshop. Why is this? Probably because planning is seen as solely an obsession of management. Blank account plans are handed out, a workshop day is arranged and perhaps a consultant arrives to give instruction. The next day it is back to normality. If you know that account plans do not drive your business, do not waste your time and that of the sales team. If you really believe that the account plan is vital to growing and controlling your key accounts, make the plan a central part of any discussions, targeting and forecasting. Do not ask for the plan to be filled with all sorts of information not directly relevant to closing business. It is a lean, efficient tool to help the sales team increase the chances of success.

There is another way to make the plan relevant and effective. Write it with the customer. This is a bit radical and cannot be done without a lot of thought. If you are encouraging your team to build their customer relationships up to the status of partnership, then building the plan with the customer makes sense. You might like to discuss this with your team. It would test those who think they are close to the customer and believe they are in partnership. If they are right, then to jointly create a plan with the customer would give excellent influence and long term business.

The Territory Plan

In many sales environments, the sales person does not have a few big accounts but many small ones. The account plan becomes a territory plan. Here, the objective is to ensure the effort goes where it will be most effective. It is helpful to divide the accounts in the territory into four bands, Active, Passive, Casual, and Unknown.

Active Those which provide a good level of business or have the potential to do so.

Passive Accounts worth visiting for steady business but are not expected to grow.

Casual Poor or infrequent business and not worth visiting. These accounts should not be ignored as, taken together, they can represent a large part of your revenue. It is better to consider lower cost methods of selling. Telesales and direct marketing can be effective.

Unknown Prospects where you do not have sufficient information to classify them.

The territory plan is designed to provide a good level of contact with Active accounts and some contact with Passive accounts. The information on each account can be the minimum necessary to forecast business and plan the visit or contact plan. It will vary across industries but below is a possible minimum.

Address
Nature of Business
Main contact
Back up contact
Revenue history – current year, previous year
Target for year
Visit frequency

Once a plan is filled in for each account, it is possible to judge if it all makes sense. The target for each account should add up to the total target, or, say, 90% allowing the Casual accounts to fill the remaining 10%. The visit frequency can be seen to be achievable or not.

The territory plan should be done mainly by the sales person but with much input by yourself. You must have a view on both the minimum revenue required to keep a sales person on the road and how you want to grow the business. If the plan does not deliver, then you need to work on it until it does.

5 New business

It is tough getting new business. It needs a different approach and the sales person has to have more resilience and resolve. While it would be convenient to concentrate all new business on one sales person or team, the fact is that most sales people need to do some. Even the existing account manager needs to make new contacts and try to take a bigger share from any competitors.

It is in this type of selling that sales and marketing come close together. Sales and marketing were looked at in an earlier chapter so here we will take the output from marketing and form a sales plan around it. It could be that you operate in a well defined market and you know the relevant prospects that you have not yet approached. You can go straight to sales tactics. If not, then you need to be methodical and form a sales plan. This sales plan can incorporate the account or territory plan in due course. What you want to achieve is a plan that you can agree with the sales person. The plan will only be as good as the market research you can afford in time and money. You could just hire a sales person with experience in the market you want to enter. This is a sensible route but you need to know enough to hire the right person and then set the appropriate targets and goals.

So, how to do this? There are so many markets and approaches that trying to form a general method may not be very useful. Instead we will look at a particular situation to establish the principals. Suppose you were in the construction industry and had developed a new product. It sold well but you needed new markets to increase manufacturing volume. It looked likely that the water industry could use the product as it had major advantages over the present methods. You have no contacts or experience in the water industry and are relying on the opinion of a contact in a regular customer. As your sales force is fully stretched, the only way forward is to hire a new sales person and get that person to open up the market.

You have a number of critical issues to face and some hard work to do. If you run a small business, there is not much room for mistakes. At this stage you want to achieve a simple plan that makes sense. The key points are:

- Is the market big enough to justify the investment?
- Is the product a good fit?
- Who do you sell to and how many of them are there?
- What kind of sales person is required?
- What should the sales person do and what should be the targets?

If you go to a bookshop, you will find the shelves groaning with the weight of books on marketing, business planning and market research. There is no point in repeating all that here. It is assumed that you have taken on the task of analysing the market or delegated it to someone else. Let us then look at each point in turn.

- **Is the market big enough to justify the investment?**

Your product is for waste water treatment. You find that there are a fixed number of water companies in the UK and each has many waste water treatment plants. In fact, there are hundreds of potential sites spread all over the country. Each site could use several of the new products. You add the numbers and the result is very encouraging. You note that the spread of companies appears to be even across the country with little concentration in particular areas.

- **Is the product a good fit?**

Your product offers good energy saving and a longer life. It would appear to replace the existing products with minimal disruption. You judge the risk of changing is small.

- **Who do you sell to and how many of them are there?**

This is where it gets tricky. The water companies do not necessarily design and install the equipment. They often use independent contractors and engineering consultants. The engineers at the waste sites would not change the supplier or design without authority. Also these people are not interested in efficiency, only maintenance. You find out how many contractors or water design companies there are. There are quite a lot, big and small with no way of knowing who are the ones to target. The water companies, at a senior level, are interested in efficiency and cost saving. It is down to the independent contractors to deliver it.

- **What kind of sales person is required?**

At first you thought you needed someone to go round hundreds of water treatment sites offering the new product – a combination of direct mail and foot slogging. It is clear that that strategy will not work. It would have been money and effort wasted. In fact, you want a more strategic sales person, able to sell the benefits of energy saving at senior levels in the water companies. At the same time the sales person must find out which contractors the target water companies will potentially use to install the new product. A second level sell will be required at the contractors to convince them that the new product is a viable solution. The sales person must therefore be comfortable with selling total cost of ownership benefits at senior levels. This sales person should also be comfortable with the concept of selling to critical decision makers who are not the buyers and then selling to buyers in a different company who may be resistant to change. In fact, to be successful, a senior sales person is required, not necessarily with water industry experience but with a combination of engineering and finance skills.

- **What should the sales person do and what should be the targets?**

You have decided that the key to success is to have at least one of your products in each water company. The savings will be obvious and will lead naturally to more orders. The plan for the sales person will focus on reference sites in targeted water companies. You will not reward with a commission based on revenue but will give a bonus for each reference site installed and running. This will be the objective for the first year. In the second year, there will be a commission based on revenue to encourage further sales, plus bonuses based on new reference sites.

As sales manager, you would probably provide the new sales person with a Sales Agreement based on the template at the beginning of this chapter. Under management objectives included would be a requirement to create account plans for a minimum number of water companies and associated contractors. In the section on compensation would be the bonus structure paid on the creation of reference sites. The sales person now knows what to do and how to be rewarded. You will have done enough research on the market to have created a structure for the sales person which defines success and the route to achieve success.

Hopefully, you can now turn your attention to other matters. Unfortunately, as in most situations, nothing goes smoothly and the progress of the sales person may dictate changes to the plan. The plans are not sacred and must reflect a combination of the possible and desirable. The important point is that you have a plan; it outlines what you want and how to measure progress. Without the steps taken above, you may have employed the wrong type of sales person and not accurately defined a successful sales campaign.

6 The sales meeting

The sales meeting will take up at least half a day of prime selling time. You really do need to understand why you do it or valuable time will be wasted and never recovered. I suggest that sales meetings are useful – but only for a limited range of reasons. The three most important are to inform, share and encourage. Before looking at these it is worthwhile dismissing the typical reasons for having sales meetings that are a waste of time.

Don't do it – 1

Don't ask each sales person for a forecast. Going round each team member for a laborious resume of business is mind numbing for the rest of the team and wastes their time. Do it individually, outside the meeting and before the meeting.

Don't do it – 2

Don't use the meeting to show up poor performers or humiliate anyone. These issues are tackled individually.

Don't do it – 3

Don't show everyone you are the boss. If you are, you are.

If the above is what you do *not* do, what then do you do? For each sales person, you have a sales agreement that states what is expected of them. The forecasting tells you the possible results. The reporting is a view on how they are doing and the plans set out the how they go about it. What is left for the sales meeting? The sales meeting is to build a team and, if done well, the result is greater than the sum of the parts. Here are some suggestions of what the meeting could contain.

Sales figures

The overall company sales figures are important and so is how they compare with the business plan. It may be appropriate to list the numbers for each sales person and show how they add up to the total. Not every team member may be measured on revenue so you need to think through, why and how you display the results. If it is to show up the laggards, just remember that dealing with problems of performance is best done outside the meeting. If you are over plan then congratulate; under plan then investigate. You are looking for solutions, not whinges or sloping shoulders. Be careful that any numbers you put up are accurate. This goes back to whether you can rely on your systems.

Reports

The sales meeting is a good forum to share information and experience. The problem is usually how to do it without getting bogged down by the obsessed, the pedants, the irrelevant and the doom merchants. It is tempting to give each team member a period of time to summarise points of interest. If you have a disciplined team able to succinctly deliver nuggets of wisdom gleaned from experience, then congratulations, just go ahead. You might be better off making your own summary compiled from reports and ask for comments. Unless what is discussed is relevant to the whole team, you are using prime selling time to numb the bum and brain.

Strategy

This is the time to restate or modify the company strategy. Sales people need to know what their company stands for and where it is going. Do not assume that they know it. If they do not know it, then neither will their customers.

Plan

Key events such as exhibitions and marketing initiatives need to be decided and resourced. Anything you do to get leads will be wasted unless you are well prepared to act and act promptly. Your sales team are well placed to give good feedback on marketing spend.

Inform

Guest speakers can be extremely useful and add real value to your meeting. They can be from your own company, partner companies, customers, professional services such as legal and so on. Internecine battles can be eased by this kind of communication. Ask the hated manager of Credit Control to explain to your team why their customers can be put on credit hold and how they can help. Maybe someone from legal who can tell them how they can avoid going to jail or get the company fined. It is all about broadening the knowledge of the team so they can get things right first time.

Reward

This is the place to congratulate and hand out rewards and so on. A popular one is *Sales Person of the Month* or similar. Do not just give a prize to the sales person who got the most orders. This will quickly be resented as there is hardly a level playing field out there. Reward ingenuity, perseverance, imagination or any other personal characteristic that can act as a role model.

At the end of the sales meeting your team should be better informed and encouraged than before. This is easy enough if times are good. If sales are down and the outlook is difficult, work through the content of the meeting with more care. You are the boss so you should have the plan and the strategy. You have the core information from reports and forecasts. You can sound out ideas with individuals before the meeting. The meeting must result in a united team who know where they are going and what they must do. If you do not achieve this, you have wasted your time (and theirs).

9

How to Manage the Team

This is the crunch chapter. Everything learnt so far will be brought together with leadership and management skills so as to make your sales team a force in the land. You now have a structure for the sales team and all the processes and systems are in place. You should though, think of them as buoys, lighthouses and other navigation aids. They are reference points to provide structure and boundaries for the team. They are not the system of management because, if they were, then a computer could replace you and no one would notice.

The previous chapters have concentrated on detailed management rather than leadership. Time now to add *leadership* to the processes and systems in order to generate business. There is no simple system or strategy that combines leadership, management, process and structure. Running a sales department is too complex, so all the devices and attributes above have to be used separately or together to mould your team into an efficient, effective and determined team. It is no use describing this in theory with carefully chosen examples. The only way is to get to the coalface of selling and go through a whole selling cycle and meet the issues head on. It is rare to find simple answers and obvious directions in most selling environments. You will, at times, be a leader, perhaps a mentor, simply a sounding board, or an additional senior sales person. Your team will regard you in the same way, perhaps with the addition of 'pedantic sod, obstructionist, control freak and mister meeting'.

While it is fashionable to be a leader, leadership and management have their distinct place. Setting the style, culture, vision and drive of a department or company is leadership. Making things work day by day is management. If you have both and do not confuse them, you will be a power in the land. To illustrate this, I have combined in this chapter the generation of motivation and the daily business of selling. Motivation is down to leadership. The rest is management.

Motivation

Every employer wants the staff to be motivated. It makes management so much easier, customers sense the enthusiasm and having staff wanting to go the extra mile helps growth and productivity. Too often it remains merely something desirable and to be dealt with when there is time. Strangely, in some organisations, high motivation seems to be there anyway without anyone consciously whipping it up.

Considering how desirable and welcome motivation is to any company, it is surprising how little real analysis and effort most organisations devote to it. In sales departments, motivation is vital and, for sales-led businesses, lack of motivation can have a significant effect on performance and staff retention. Given the importance of rule number one defined in the previous chapter – *measure what people achieve, not what they do day to day* – motivation is a key driver if you want your team to get up and do their job enthusiastically.

Generating motivation is not a quick fix but something to be built into the ethos of the company. It will not happen overnight but needs to be built up step-by-step, based on large and small decisions and actions. You may be tempted to go on a motivation course, or even send the team. Being wound up into a frenzy by a hyperactive motivation expert is good fun. Finish the evening with an Indian or Chinese meal, a few lagers and get a taxi home. Sadly, when you get into the office the next morning, nothing will have changed. The advice and slogans, which seemed so important the day before, will have evaporated with the hangover.

People are motivated, firstly, when they believe in what they do and who they work for, and secondly, when they believe that the organisation believes in them and values them as individuals. You can have one of the above and not the other but it is best to have both. This is why one-day motivation courses are hugely enjoyable but a waste of time. In fact, the best time to go on one is when the team is heaving with motivation and deserves a day out.

Take the first requirement for motivation. The most motivated employees are proud of who they work for. The company may have a famous brand name or be small and local. Whichever it is, the organisation must represent values that an employee can identify with. If the name or brand suggests values that transcend just product details, employees feel ownership of those values and feel that, they too, as individuals, reflect those values. If you are chatting to someone at a party who works for, say, the BBC or IBM, you will be told very quickly. Being employed by these organisations conveys status based on quality and competence. Past employees of Enron or Andersons may be less forthcoming about their CV.

The second is more difficult. Most organisations make rather pious statements about valuing their employees. It is a delicate balancing act to push them hard enough to earn their keep while keeping the good ones satisfied enough not to walk into another job. The stick and carrot approach is difficult to get right when times are good. In an economic downturn, it is common to hit them with the carrot when the stick breaks.

How then to get your sales force motivated? A well-motivated sales force will have more effect than a well-motivated any other department. They are largely free of direct day-to-day management control and are knowledge workers whose knowledge needs to be willingly released. The first point to be made is that organisations with well-motivated staff are not shy. They promote themselves with vigour. Whether it is quality of service, the fastest product, the freshest food; if you want to motivate your staff tell them and anyone else just how good your company is. Sales people want to believe in what they are doing. Even if things go wrong, they want to believe that the issues will be fixed. How will your sales staff go that bit further if they think their offering or organisation is only average? Work at this and if it seems that your business is only average, do something about it. In so many ways, unless you aim to fly with the eagles you will walk with the turkeys. Your organisation needs an ethos so that people are proud to work for it. If you are the owner or sales manager, you need to constantly reinforce your advantages or superlatives from the competition. Your sales people must believe that who they are and what they sell are somehow special. This is not just for your sales staff; all employees want to feel proud of what they do. But, sales people have to tell others as well.

This issue is really about marketing. While we think of marketing as a way of promoting awareness in your market sector, it should not be forgotten that internal marketing also has a vital role. When your sales people are given promotional literature, data sheets or any other customer-focused information, are they impatient to give them to customers? Is there a wow factor? Also, internal information should articulate why the product or service is special. This does not mean lies or mis-information. If the task is not possible and your product or service is just average or mediocre, then maybe you will have to accept an average sales force, as keen to go home as to see a customer.

Let us assume that your company does have something special and you are engaged in making sure everyone knows about it. The sales force believe they have a winner and are keen to sell. How then do we tackle the second point of motivation and show that each person is valued? Much has been said and done on this issue and, generally, more said than done. It is not the intention of this book to labour the sociology and psychology of people and work. Even if there was a chapter on the subject in this book, the brutal truth is that most owners and managers have too much to do without a bout of navel gazing. Not only that, but the issue has been over-complicated by a trend to treat motivation as another company process to be rolled out by HR.

Fortunately, there is a simple and uncomplicated motivation strategy that the most modest businesses can follow. In this chapter and elsewhere in the book where people management is concerned, commitments are given and rewards offered in response. Make the commitments fair and reasonable and do not short change on the rewards. Maintain frequent and open dialogue and, occasionally, give a reward without being asked. Does this sound too simple? Surely there is more to it than that? There is probably more to be made of it, if desired, but you have a business to run and no time to waste. The real issue about motivation and being valued is one of trust. Employees will feel valued if they know that any commitments made will be honoured. Sales people are particularly sensitive to this. Those who are remote from the office need contact and reassurance. If you want any of the sales team to go the extra mile, the effort should not be taken for granted and forgotten soon after. Making the sales team feel valued need cost no more money or take more time. It is a matter of approach and judgement. Get it right and your team is ready to go, excited by what they are selling and motivated to move mountains.

There is another route to what many companies consider as motivation. Pay lots of money to the successful and sack the ones who do not deliver. A bit harsh, but it is common in many organisations. It is not, of course, motivation in the way described in this book, just greed and fear. Ultimately it will cost more in both money and company performance.

Managing the selling cycle

This is the day-to-day business for the company owner or sales manager. You can read any number of books on leadership and strategy and none will help on all those decisions, great or detailed, which have to be made every working hour. The grand strategy can be overtaken by events; your best sales person suddenly resigns; the competition slashes their prices; you ask a sales person a simple question, 'When will you get an order from XYZ Ltd?' (The answer leaves you none the wiser and you remember that you asked the same question last month. The order was promised for last week but there is no sign of it.) The first three events are beyond this book but the last will be tackled firmly.

Selling is not a black art. If it was, sales forecasting would be a branch of clairvoyancy and that is certainly not the case. The trouble is that selling has gained a reputation for equating success with poorly defined but crucial personal skills. These include the silver tongue, miraculous closing techniques, manipulation and 'the buyer owes me one'. A company owner, perhaps with no sales background, may find it difficult to get a satisfactory statement on the progress, or lack of progress, of an order.

Buying and selling is not a mystery, though the reasons people buy and sell may, sometimes, defy logic. There is a distinct process to go through which can vary only in the number of steps and speed. Ignoring the extremes, most buying and selling can be fairly well defined. This was touched on in the previous chapter when forecasting was described. Accurate forecasting requires knowledge of the logical steps that a buyer will go through. To this buying cycle, there is a corresponding selling cycle. The selling cycle is usually based on the buying cycle and the selling strategy is based on anticipating the needs of the buying cycle. All you need to do is define and understand the typical buying cycle for your industry.

Now, far from being bamboozled by a scarcely coherent explanation of the possibility of an order, you can ask specific questions and get expect specific answers. This will allow you to manage, add value and predict future business without a crystal ball or a random number generator.

First we will look at the buying cycle.

The buying cycle

From buying a chair to planning a new power station, buying is a step-by-step process. The steps may be repeated, more can be added, maybe one taken out, but there is always a process. An order can only be placed when the last step is taken so, know which step the buyer is on, and you stand a chance of knowing when the last step will be taken.

The steps can be given different names or even sub-divided but they will not stray too far from the ones below.

- Be aware of need
- Qualify need
- Investigate the market

- Ask for bids
- Compare bids
- Select preferred supplier

Let us take a look at each step to see what they mean.

Be aware of need

A capital spend or requirement for a service can arise in many ways. Competitive pressure, change in the law, need to improve manufacturing margins and simple expansion. Out-sourcing of non-core activities is popular to improve service where there is a lack of company expertise. A big contract could be won and new suppliers are to be considered. Some of these needs are really problems that are widely discussed or even commented on in an annual report. Others could be secret and circulated only within senior management. Whether it is a multi-million pound manufacturing line or a new kitchen, the project champion will keep the need alive until it finds support.

Qualify need

At some point, a need or project takes on more substance. It will require quantifying in various terms such as cost, payback, timescale and resource. One or more people will be allocated to the task and it will become visible to a wide selection of others. The type of solution will be determined in outline, probably from previous experience but new ideas could be welcomed. If the cost is unknown or not budgeted, then ensuring viability could be crucial. Existing suppliers will be contacted for pricing. This process could be on the legendary back of a fag packet or a detailed exercise. Whichever it is, at some point, someone or a committee, perhaps the board, will decide whether to take it further. If it looks good, a budget could be set and the action starts.

Investigate market

This is the point when the project goes public. Unless the solution is simple, or a repeat of previous practice, the customer will do some serious work with potential suppliers. The customer may have one or several objectives or outcomes. If the solution is not fixed or complex, the budget may not be set. Getting the money is usually a defining moment and what may look like a straightforward procurement exercise is actually a phoney war. The outcome is not an order but confirmation of cost; then, the whole exercise begins again, this time for real. This is the time to look at new suppliers who may have keener prices or a different approach. The buyer is in a very powerful position and can use this investigation process to wind up and pressurise existing suppliers. Often, the result of this stage is a detailed specification or tender document.

Ask for bids

The preparation should now have been done, the budget has been agreed, the best type of solution has been specified and possible suppliers have been identified. In the Public Sector, large bids have to follow a defined route; the requirement will need to be placed in the European Journal. This is to improve competition in the European Union by making the process open and public. It is a good idea, in theory, but the efforts of both customers and suppliers up to this point will have roughed up the level playing field.

The specification may call for a simple quotation or a substantial proposal. While the private sector has the choice of how competitive to make the process, a good buyer will not let pass the opportunity to secure the best deal. The threat of opening the project to competition may just do the trick. A more forceful tactic will be to ask for several bids but structure them to ensure a desired outcome. The bid list could include the favourite, a good alternative, a wildcard (possibly to keep the price keen), and a supplier all the other bidders hate.

Compare bids

The bids or quotations are received formally or informally depending on the legalities of the process. The customer will assess the bids by a range of methodologies from a precise, legalistic scoring system to a casual, cryptic, 'our usual supplier seems to be OK again'. During this time, the suppliers will be putting on pressure by phone or dropping in as they 'were in the area'. This is the time to squeeze the suppliers in a reverse auction. A best and final offer could be requested when it is judged that the process has run its course. At some point, a winner is agreed, or at least a preferred option. The next stage could be the placing of a formal order, then again, maybe not.

Select preferred supplier

While it could be that the hopeless bids have gone in the dustbin, and an order faxed to the lucky supplier, there is the opportunity to squeeze a bit harder to get a better deal. It is possible that at least one of the other bids has been left on the table and this bid is, according to the customer, a credible alternative. With an order tantalisingly close, it take a brave or confident sales person to stand firm against any erosion of profit in the order. For the buyer, this is the time to get some additional concessions. An invitation to discuss terms and conditions can means stress and trouble all round. Finally the buyer agrees to give a firm written order and the process is finished.

Anyone who has bought a car or a new kitchen has gone through the steps above and it is little different for a guided missile. The complexities of the product or service can hide the logical, straightforward steps and some purchases are so simple that it could be thought that they do not apply. They certainly do and anyone managing sales people needs to be aware of the buying cycle. This is particularly important for business owners who may not employ a dedicated sales manager. While an experienced sales manger may get quickly to the heart of a sales campaign going off the rails, the non-specialist may just get bogged down in detail and the sales person's lack of focus.

So, how does a sales person find out about the customer buying cycle? There is no mystery about this; the sales person asks the customer. It helps if it is an existing customer and there is an account plan in place. Account plans were covered in detail in the previous chapter. The plan should name the key contacts, their position, role and influence. Asking the right questions to as many people as possible will establish the buying cycle. At the early stages, there could be different views on the viability of any project, whether it will happen and if it will be funded. Later, it is surprising how difficult it can be to pin down the real decision makers. Making sense of ambiguous information is the job of the sales person and making sure it is done is the job of sales management.

Before looking at the selling cycle it is worth clarifying your role in the cut and thrust of winning the orders. If you do not add value, you add very little of use. Remember rule number one; if you have to tell your team what to do you might as well do it yourself. As they are out of the office most of the time, doing the job alone, you must support them, advise them, mentor them and, as no one is perfect, correct them. Leadership is the style you adopt; management is the mechanics of the process. If you do not feel you are up to it, get training or other help. It's lonely up there; few people around you will volunteer an honest opinion.

The selling cycle

An order may arrive on the fax machine but, as can be seen above, it does not arrive by magic. It is the culmination of much work, some of which is visible to the sales person. For the sales person, the task is not just to know the current position on the buying cycle but also to sell appropriate to that position. The buying cycle has a corresponding selling cycle that also has an order and logic associated with it. In general, the sales person has limited control over the buying cycle. Depending on the competition, control over the selling cycle may be limited as well. This is an area of management that is fraught with difficulties. It is natural and tempting for the sales manager to use what information there is to tell the sales person what to do. This breaks rule number one. On the other hand, using the selling cycle to question the sales person can uncover skills or competence issues that may need addressing. Yes, it is difficult, but then, this book never said that the job of the sales manager is easy.

Just as with the buying cycle, it is easy to think that selling cycles vary widely. But, like the buying cycle, they follow a pattern and the steps below are a good summary.

- Identify interest
- Influence outcome
- Qualify opportunity
- Assess the competition and submit proposal
- Discuss proposal
- Close the deal

The buying cycle and the selling cycle are like gears meshing together. Usually the buying cycle drives the selling cycle. It is less common for the selling cycle to drive unless the product or service is outstanding or special offer conditions are good enough to take control. The cycles take on a natural speed governed by complexity and the culture of the buyer. Tensions can arise when one party wants to move at a different speed from the other. This usually means the sales person wanting to speed up the order or the buyer wants to slow down. Sales managers and business owners are apt to pressure the sales person to get the business in before the end of the month or quarter. Sometimes it just is not possible and you need to understand why.

Taking the steps of the selling cycle in turn we will look at them from the sales manager's point of view.

Identify interest

The earlier a sales person can identify a new project or opportunity, the better the chance of winning the deal. The account manager for an existing customer is well placed to hear of a lucrative initiative being casually discussed. He or she will have a head start over any competitor who is not in the account. A good account plan should have identified possible openings for new business and the relevant people. Even if the customer has not initiated the project, the sales person can do it. An unsolicited proposal carefully thought out and targeted at the right person can be very effective.

For the new business sales person, there are difficulties in getting in at the start of new projects before they go public. They are working more blind than an established account manager and so need to be more methodical and focused in finding out what is going on. Correct targeting is essential to avoid much wasted time.

The sales manager wants to see a steady pipeline of business covering some considerable number of weeks or months into the future. Sales people with good performing accounts can lapse into picking low hanging fruit as it is so much easier. Too much of this and the apparently safe account becomes a happy hunting ground for any competitor. Questioning the sales person about possible embryonic projects can lead to the assertion that there are none. Be very sceptical unless the sales person is one you can trust. Use the account plan to drive activity and identify potential areas for business. It is at this point that it becomes clear whether the sales person has a wide enough range of contacts. New projects that are likely to be funded emerge at more senior management levels. If there is no contact at this level, then it is probable that the sales person finds out about the project at the same time as a competitor. Worse, your sales person finds out about a project from too low a level of contact by which time it has gone public and the chance to quietly influence has evaporated.

Manager's checklist

- Is there a good pipeline of prospects or projects?
- Is the account plan being used to uncover or generate projects?
- Is the sales activity productive in identifying projects and prospects?

Influence outcome

What was just a possible project now takes on some substance. With an existing customer, this is the time to ensure that any solution is as close as possible to the offerings of the sales person. In many instances, when a tender or specification is read through, the fingerprints of a competitor are all over it. It is at this point in the project that it happens. The specification is being considered and can be vulnerable to different or novel solutions. For the competent sales person, all that hard work in customer satisfaction and making contacts should now be rewarded. It is important to know if the project has gone public at this point. If not, and customer satisfaction is high, then there is the opportunity to cut a deal and not go through the stress and aggravation of open competition. In a large public sector procurement, there is no choice but to go to the market. However, nothing is completely fair and the good account manager will be working hard to load the dice.

If a new business sales person comes across the opportunity, then some quick work is necessary. Is it an open opportunity and worth investing time and effort? It is easy to be encouraged to bid and simply be used to beat up the existing supplier for a better deal. Can the goal posts be moved to disadvantage the existing supplier?

For the sales manager, this is the first point that a sales campaign can be monitored and forecast in a meaningful way. While the revenue values and timings may be difficult to judge, the project will have some substance in relevance and intent. However, the mortality rate for projects at this stage is high and a sales manager will like to see several to ensure solid business for the future.

This stage in the selling cycle will tell the sales manager how deeply an account manager type sales person knows the customer. A sales person who is approached by a main board director to comment on a new project or development is at the pinnacle of the profession. They are worth every penny you pay them. If, on the other hand, the first sign of business is a request for a quote or an entry in the European Journal then the sales person has no idea of what is going on. The account plan should be inspected to check the range and seniority of the listed contacts. The sales person may need help to climb the hierarchy in a major company. This is not an easy task and the sales manager may need to decide if the sales person can benefit from the investment of time in skills training. Some people have a natural ceiling in how far they can be developed in a role. Rather than seeing the sales person as failing, that person may in fact do an excellent job with a different profile of customer.

There is another consideration that puts a responsibility for action on the sales manager or business owner. Depending on the customer, there can be a barrier to how far up the customer hierarchy a sales person can go. An old rule of thumb is that the range of movement for a sales person is one below and one above their equivalent level in the customer's organisation. As organisations flatten and become less formal, this rule has become more flexible. However, it could be that to move up to board of director level, a more senior person, such as yourself, as sales manager or business owner, has to get involved with making that call.

If your sales person is competent and in control, you can move on to discuss the next forecasted project. Anything less than competent and you should check that a plan is in place to track the opportunity. The plan could include ensuring the sales person has appropriate contacts, knowledge of timescales, and the ability to feed the customer with such suggestions and information to bias the project in your favour. In the private sector, this is the time to decide whether to make a pre-emptive bid, grabbing the business before it attracts the competition. It may not be possible to precisely size the potential and risk at this stage but, if the level of contact is suitable, a suggestion of a favourable deal can be made. Unless you have a reliable sales person you will need to be involved. If the customer wants to ensure a competitive bid, then showing your hand early may not be wise. Also, you could give away more than necessary. Account and contact knowledge is vital for these decisions.

The new business sales person has to decide at this stage whether to pursue the opportunity or drop it and move on. The sales manager is looking for two main sales-person-problem characteristics here. The first is an unrealistic expectation of success. Most sales people are optimists, like gamblers, but the best reduce the odds of failure. A possible big opportunity can cloud the judgement. There has to be evidence that the procurement is open, or at least, a genuine competitor stands a chance. A major sales campaign takes time, energy and resources. Serious effort in one place means no effort somewhere else. You may have to tell the sales person to disengage unless you are satisfied that success is possible. The other problem is the search for low hanging fruit. It could be that you hired the sales person to develop an industry or a selection of accounts. It may be new territory or possibly neglected for some time. You know instinctively that there is business to be gained. After a time, the sales person has a short pipeline or reports little business. Is there really little business or is your new sales person only looking for quick sales with little effort? Are these accounts being skimmed rather than dug? This is a tough one. You rely on the sales person giving you accurate information and informed opinion. It could be, even after diligently following this book, that you have hired a dog. This was covered in a previous chapter on what happens when it all goes wrong. Let us assume for now that the sales person is suitable. Behaviour is set by expectation and reward. If you are convinced that concentrated effort will yield business, check the sales agreement again. Is it written in a way that does not reflect the task you want done? Work through the accounts that should have potential and agree a programme of actions that should uncover some business. Does your sales person have some skill shortages? For instance, confidence with the telephone is important in new business. Consider such specific skills training.

With less account knowledge than the incumbent supplier, decision making in new business is difficult. New business sales people are a rather special breed. They work harder, do more real selling and need to have awesome resilience. They are often under-valued as it is common to bring in smaller value orders as they gain a foothold in accounts. Larger selling organisations tend to reward the sales people who bring in the biggest deals. Hence the old adage, 'who is the best sales person?'... answer, 'the one with the best accounts'. If you are serious about new business, get the right attitude towards it.

Manager's Checklist

- Is the opportunity relevant?
- Should it be pursued?
- Is it being tracked carefully?
- Can the sales person handle it alone?

Qualify opportunity

At some point, an opportunity turns serious, the race starts, there is one winner and no second place. The stage starts with making final the previous preparations. If a specification is to be written, this is the last chance to influence it. A budget could be set. Someone, probably in a senior position, owns the project and may, or may not, be the final decision maker. In the public sector, the entry for the European Journal will be prepared.

The second part of this step is the actual approval of the specification, contact with suppliers or appearance of the project in the European Journal. Sometimes the move to buying from just collecting information can be difficult to judge. In less structured buying departments, there is always the possibility of a quick deal, possibly by a competitor. Here, information you supplied supposedly in advance of a more formal request to quote may be used to discard your company from a shortlist you never knew existed. As usual, keeping close to the key contacts is crucial.

Unless the response to the specification is a simple quotation, then real work and resources will be used to pursue this deal to the end. Again, a competent sales person will make this judgement and perhaps use the sales manager as a sounding board. Up to now, the assumption has been made that you, as manager, will let the competent get on with their job and only check and actively manage the less then competent to a degree related to their abilities. Unfortunately, few sales managers can keep out of a deal when it gets to the interesting stage. The control freak manager can harm a relationship with a good sales person by getting involved without adding value. Typically, a business owner wants to have some control without having the necessary experience. A sales manager may want to prove that all the old selling skills are still in place. It is difficult for such managers to understand that a good sales person will use them as strategic resource in a sales campaign for particular tasks. Being used rather than controlling can take some getting used to. It is an attitude of mind thing. You have to believe that your task is to help the sales person to be successful and that may include not giving instructions but receiving them.

Unfortunately, not all your team will be formidable selling machines. It is at this stage in the selling cycle that your account manager sales person can reach the peak of complacency rather than selling prowess. It is a good idea to test and qualify the opportunity at this point rather than be caught out later. There are a number of systems devised to qualify opportunities by scoring points. None are foolproof, but are useful in highlighting the key factors in accessing the strength of the position of a supplier. Any potential business of a size that would soak up considerable resource should be discussed as objectively as possible. Often, a sales person is not as objective as desirable when contemplating a large order. Even if the business is winnable, it may cost more than it is worth. Unless your sales person is a guarantor for your overdraft, you may have reasons for questioning the deal that do not resonate with a hungry account manager.

Here is an example of a qualifying checksheet.

Name of Project

____

		Score
Is the project a good fit?	(Yes 5, No –10)	__
Standard products and services?	(Yes 0, No –5)	__
Are we a preferred supplier?	(Yes 5, No –5)	__
Have we discussed project at board level?	(Yes 10, No 0)	__
Is there known competition?	(Yes 0, No 5)	__
Will there be penalty conditions?	(Yes –2, No 0)	__
Will there be special payment terms?	(Yes –5, No 0)	__
Standard terms and conditions of sale?	(Yes 0, No –5)	__
Normal delivery times?	(Yes 0, No –5)	__
Total		___

The exact criteria will depend on your business as will the scoring method. It is tempting to state a cut off score, below which the bid will be abandoned. There is no reason to be pedantic in applying the system. A score may be poor but there may be reasons for putting forward a bid which you consider you cannot win. With existing accounts, this is common and you will at least move forward clear in what you are doing and the reasons why. In the same way, a score may be good but with one consideration giving rise to such misgiving that it affects the whole.

Some sales people like filling in forms and being very analytical in assessing business. They are suspiciously adept at spreadsheets and collect data like a squirrel collects nuts. Very laudable and efficient but just make sure they do the basic sales groundwork and do not pull the wool over your eyes. At the other extreme are the have-car-will-travel, flying Dutchmen who despise paperwork, controls, assessment and accounting to anyone for their time. It is in qualifying bids using both logic and good customer information that a manager needs to get a grip on both types. You can fill in as many forms as you can devise but, at the final analysis, the decision will be based on a subjective assessment of 'is it winnable and do we want to win it?' It is all down to the quality of sales work and the information collected from it.

So why is this the point of maximum complacency for the account manger? It is probable that the specification is, at least, an acceptable fit for the company product. The normal contacts have been met, lunched and, unless there is an issue, would have sounded accommodating. If competition was not mentioned, then the sales person would be unlikely to raise it. No point in putting ideas into their minds. However, a touch of paranoia is an intrinsic part of the consistently successful sales person. If members of your sales team do not show any paranoia, you need some on their behalf. Ask the difficult questions. Whether you accept the answers depends on how you rate the sales people. It is at this point that slack account management with a narrow range of contacts and few at the right levels will prove the Achilles' heel of the sales campaign.

It is vital that the outcome of this stage of the buying cycle is known. There are a number of possibilities. The following are some.

- A firm specification to bid against. Very probable in the public sector after an entry in the European Journal.

- A willingness to consider an offer to snap up the business before the process goes any further.
- A competitor has been quietly working on the account and puts in a pre-emptive bid at a special price or conditions to get a foot in the door.

This is not a book on sales tactics but the manager needs to know that all eventualities are covered. You will never know everything and decisions are based on best judgement. It does not stop you from asking the questions though.

The new business sales person works to different pressures. The sales manager wants the sales person to both avoid hopeless causes and grasp the difficult but possible. Less opportunity to influence the specification reduces the likelihood of a good fit. It may happen to be good enough to consider other issues. Would a competitive bid just be used to beat up the incumbent supplier? This is a tough one and a good reason why the failure rate for new business selling is high. Can an alternative be made sufficiently appealing? Cut the price? Offer more for the same money? Is your alternative so novel and the benefits potentially so great that the customer will take a risk? Could the incumbent be out-flanked by a sneak bid making an offer that cannot be matched? A qualifying checksheet can be used for new business in the same way as for the account manager. It has to take account of the greater risk involved, not just for the seller but the customer as well.

While an account manager may chase an opportunity buoyed up by complacency, a new business sales person may use an opportunity to cover a thin pipeline in real business. As mentioned before, it is a tough call for a manager to tell a sales person to drop a deal and move on. There is often little hard evidence to decide that a bid would definitely win or fail. This is the last opportunity to call a halt before being sucked into a commitment of resources. The manager is working with data collected by the sales person. Fact and fiction can merge seamlessly in the right hands. It is usually at this point that a joint visit is suggested. Some sensitivity is required here, particularly to understand why you as manager should want to visit the customer.

The joint visit

There are only two reasons to do a joint visit to the customer; (a) as part of a strategy to strengthen the selling position and (b) to check the performance of the sales person. Whichever it is, from the point of view of the customer, it must be seen as part of the selling process. Any competent buyer will spot the performance-check visit and will treat it appropriately. If you are not comfortable with the ability of a sales person, do not make it even worse. Make the visit look like a training exercise and you will undermine your authority as well as the sales person.

There are many ways the joint visit can be made genuine even if the object is an appraisal. For instance, you could set your sales person the task of moving up the customer hierarchy. This could be enabled by asking your sales person to set up a meeting with your equivalent or one above. You also will need to do some work to get the most from the meeting. It will be wasted unless you can put on the table a suggestion, offer or programme that reflects your position in having an authority which should not be expected from the sales person. So, whether you are moving the customer along or checking your staff, the actions need to be customer related. The difference is the role taken by the sales person. With very competent staff, the role is partnership. If the visit is driven by concerns, this should be made clear to the sales person and the role tailored to address specific issues.

There are two dangers for the manager in the customer call. The first is common for managers who were red-hot sales staff. It is tempting to show how well you can sell in what becomes an ego trip rather then a customer visit. Unless you want to spend all your life selling for your staff, then resist the temptation to show how good you were. Discuss your roles before and keep to them. The other is to play the boss too hard. Customers and buyers like to see partnership and genuine support for colleagues. The more manipulative buyers will exploit any dysfunctional tendencies to their advantage. Even if you want to pull your sales person limb from limb, leave it until after the meeting.

Finally, you are at the point when you say to your sales person, 'do we go for it or what?' As a general rule, this decision should be left to the sales person. Remember rule number one. Only dictate when you have good specific reasons and they run counter to less good objections. Normally, by the time you have reached this stage, there is little debate, one way or the other. Time then, to grab the business.

Manager's Checklist

- Is the opportunity a good fit and would a bid stand a reasonable chance of success?
- Is the sales person making appropriate contacts and gaining accurate information?
- Are timescales, budget and buying criteria clear?
- Has the sales person the skills to progress the opportunity?

Assess the competition and submit proposal

Some sales people are naturally paranoid and pessimistic. They can be hard work as they pour out all the reasons why they need a lower price or other concessions to win the business. They are in the minority. Most sales people are optimists and hence will underestimate the competition and inflate their own abilities and offerings. There is little you can do about this. In fact, a touch of paranoia and optimism would be useful if they could comfortably co-exist in the same person. They can and do co-exist; just not comfortably. Your task is to ensure that the paranoid sees and reinforces any strengths and the optimistic recognises and counters the competition.

The first person who can recognise why people buy one thing rather than another, is able to package the technique in an intelligible manner and then bring it effectively to market, will be another billionaire. Until then, it is going to be just hard work and ordinary intelligent thinking. If your sales person has got to the stage where a quotation or proposal is to be written, then you should be satisfied that there are no surprises left to bite you – from your sales person or the customer.

This part of the selling cycle may be the precursor to clinching the order or to move a step closer, perhaps to getting on the shortlist. Either way, to be bounced out now would be much work wasted. It is tempting then to get heavy with any staff where you are not confident they have covered all angles. It is difficult to remember rule number one, particularly if you have been a sales person. How then to ensure that the proposal is sent to an eager and pleased recipient? There are two suggestions, one of which you should have been doing anyway. The regular reporting you implemented from the last chapter will have kept competition and product issues in the forefront of the team minds. This information can and must be shared. Discuss it regularly and have a plan to deal with real issues (i.e. not just sales persons' whinges) so that, in every sales campaign, you can ask whether they have been covered. The other is to implement a checklist to be completed for each quotation or proposal. Rarely will this be welcomed so only do it if there is a benefit that is obvious to both yourself and the team. If you do it because you are a control freak, time and effort will be wasted. Below is a sample checklist.

- Is the price known to the customer and acceptable?
- Is the competition known and countered by the proposal?
- Does the quotation/proposal contain information making it distinctive or unique?
- Is the solution known to the customer and acceptable?

Many other points could be added but resist the temptation unless they are vital. Checklists are stealth management so over-use is not recommended. Best to do your own checklist, keep it up your sleeve, and just ask the relevant questions.

There is one other issue to be addressed before moving on. It is astonishing how customers are left waiting for quotations or proposals. Nothing will happen until one is issued, let alone getting an order. Make the prompt production of quotations or equivalent a priority or, at least, to meet the customer expectations on when it will arrive. Where there is a specific and immovable deadline for the receipt of the quotation, real discipline is essential. This is common in the public sector and there is rarely any latitude. Just five minutes late and your efforts are as dust. Unless the sales person or bid team can plan the resources correctly, there will be stress, late nights and working weekends. When the battered and bloody sales person tells you the bid was delivered with one minute to spare after no sleep for two nights, moderate your admiration and check their time management. Is this harsh? It may have been a heroic endeavour but it could be bad planning. Look at it this way – what will be the quality of the document with half the brain cells asleep?

Hopefully, all is well and your well-drilled team have put in all their bids, quotations, offers, proposals and tenders in good order and on time. After the warning on checklists, here is another checklist.

Manager's Checklist

- Do the training and systems in place produce quality quotations or proposals?
- Can the sales team recognise the competition and are they able to articulate verbally and in writing the counter-strengths of their own offerings?

Discuss proposal

At the coffee machine, a smiling sales executive tells you that a massive proposal that soaked up most of your technical and legal resource for a month has made it to the shortlist. As you return to your office, another sales person is rushing out. He explains in a hurry that a customer wants to buy but needs to discuss the quotation first. After the initial warm feeling of anticipating business coming over the horizon, the paranoia returns. This book is not about sales tactics; you may have already sent all your team on the latest well-hyped, success guaranteed sales training course. This book is about running your business and this stage in the selling cycle is about what kind of business do you want. Your sales team will be under pressure and that means that you are under pressure.

The potential conflict is around how much you empower your team to use their judgement against the limits and boundaries you set to control the business. You want large, clean, profitable orders. You have a commission structure that rewards mainly the large part of those desirables but nothing else. You could get the order but lose your shirt. Do you want that? Commission will be discussed later in more detail but, remember, how you pay governs much about how people behave. How much do you trust your sales team? Do they identify with the business the same way that you do? Unless the quotation results in an order by return, you will be negotiating with the sales team as they negotiate with the customer.

The biggest issues are usually price, payment terms, guarantees and delivery. Unless you want to do the selling yourself you will leave it to the sales team to get the best deal. It is assumed that you have standard terms and conditions of sale, price lists, certain authorised discounts, limited warranty or guarantees and all are legal and may be available, at least on request, to interested parties. If your business could be done within the boundaries of these constraints then all is well. It is when you move outside these documented standards that judgement is needed and your relationship with the team gets strained.

It is rare for anything to have a fixed, accurate price attached to it and just as rare for price to be the only consideration. Hence, when a sales person insists that the price of a product needs to be reduced to get the order, there should always be, at least, a moment of hesitation. Unless you have a known and general problem with pricing, be sceptical if it seems to be the only issue. It is the easiest one to be trashed on and some buyers are just measured on the size of discounts. However, if you say no then you must be absolutely sure that the price is fair and competitive. You should then move the discussion on to discover the real cause of the problem. If you are not sure, then accurate questioning of the sales person to justify the reduction is necessary. This can get emotional so, just sticking to the facts is helpful. If the customer says the competition is cheaper, then some evidence is useful. Customers can be more unscrupulous than sales people in playing one supplier off another. If the customer just says that the budget is exceeded, look at payment options. Reducing prices is the last option of the desperate. Sell on price; live on rice, as the saying goes. The other issue about negotiating prices with the team is how open you want to be about gross or net margins. There comes a point when the margin becomes zero and you need another good reason to do business. Do you tell your team what the zero margin price is? That is up to you. As in most things in life, best to keep it simple. Stick to the price list if you can, otherwise be open.

Payment terms can be another tricky issue. Again, as with the price, is the customer just trying it on? This is not about late payers or organisations of doubtful credit-worthiness. They are a normal commercial risk. You are not a bank and if a potential customer wants to use you as one, insist that the sales person gets something back in return. This is a hidden price reduction but is more open to horse-trading. It gives the sales person scope to discuss alternative financing arrangements. Selling is a complex business and the time and expense training your team should get payback at this point. A good working knowledge of law and finance will reduce the possibility of your sales team being taken to the cleaners.

Performance guarantees, benchmarks and trials are part and parcel of certain types of sale. Some are fair and reasonable; in fact, you may be in a business where it is common and expected. It becomes an issue when it is sprung on your sales person out of the blue. If it had been spelt out in the tender document, then sharp words are needed to the sales person. In general, revenues from a sale are not recognised until there are no further liabilities on the seller. If you pay commission on revenue then you may want to introduce this principle into when commission is paid. This is not suggested as a stick to beat the sales person but it does concentrate the minds of all concerned on proper closure of business. As in payment terms, a sound knowledge of law and finance will help you and the sales team to negotiate sensibly. Be clear as to who has authority to agree non-standard terms or obligations. If you delegate because you believe in empowerment, then do it properly and trust your judgement. This is not an area where you can be half-hearted; you cannot half-delegate.

There is not a lot you can do about delivery in the majority of cases. If you do get the order, delivery is usually the most painful and common problem to hurt you. For the sales person, it is in delivery promises that desperation and optimism collide with unhappy results. Having struggled through complex and difficult negotiation on price, performance and so on, delivery is left until the end. Bad news on delivery is seen as a conspiracy by the factory. Blame falls on anyone who wants to continue a comfortable life instead of going the extra mile to save a sale. Do you support the sales team or the factory/warehouse? No easy answer here but if it causes trouble, it is your responsibility to fix it. You might remind the sales team of the need for accurate forecasting.

This part of sales management can seem the most exhausting. Making judgements on sales tactics based on slippery customer information and an uncertain assessment of the competence of sales staff can be draining. On the other hand, it is an ideal climate to develop staff and identify training needs. It will show up the difference between leadership and management. You will need both skills if you want to empower and encourage at the same time.

Manager's checklist

- Are you confident that your staff has adequate training in law, finance and negotiating skills.
- Have you set the boundaries that your staff can negotiate within?
- Is finance data confidential or will it be shared with your staff?

Close the deal

When is an order closed? A simple question with a simple answer. An order is closed when it is received in writing or electronically, complete with an order number that refers to your quotation or proposal and agrees payment at a specific point in time when your obligations are complete. Now, one of your hotshot sales staff has just burst into your office and places on your desk a large clean order conforming exactly to the definition above. Congratulations should be given in a warm glow of mutual satisfaction. The selling cycle is complete. You can deliver the goods and issue the invoice.

Unfortunately life is not always that simple. Your sales person comes into your office and is pleased to say his customer has eliminated the competitors and is only talking to your company. As an experienced manager, your heart sinks and the vision of a clean written order vanishes. You may well be asked to accept one of the following or a close variant.

- A Letter of Intent indicating the good intentions of the buyer – actions can be taken to ensure good delivery.
- Further negotiations on the final contract.
- A best and final offer. This could have happened at the previous stage, of course.

Your sales person has an order within grasp and so is potentially vulnerable to all sorts of undesirable emotions. It is important that you, at least, remember that the selling cycle is not complete and a cool head is required. Why are you in this position? As far as you are aware, your sales person submitted a comprehensive proposal, competitive negotiations have been completed and the customer requirements were clearly satisfied.

The first point is the most straightforward. A Letter of Intent is barely worth the paper it is written on. The only value it may have is in the sense of a commitment imposed on the buyer. It is down to your commercial judgement as to whether you want to accept the letter and set in train any actions you would normally take for an order. The reasons for providing a letter of intent should give a clue. If the letter is offered due to purely procedural and time consuming matters in issuing the formal order, you may feel comfortable to accept it at face value. If the reason relates to one or both of the other two points in the list above, then be very, very cautious.

Before getting to grips with the motives of the buyer, think about the sales person. Do you have a sales person who finds it difficult to ask for an order? It may seem strange, but some otherwise good sales people falter at the point when the selling is done and the customer should be pressed for the business. Perhaps, after a long campaign, this crunch point is avoided so as not to disappoint? If this situation happens frequently with a particular person, you should tackle it. It could be that skills training in assertiveness or negotiation is helpful. If you are unsure but suspect that this is the case, then a joint visit to the customer could confirm the situation.

Even if you have a sales person who can close, you may still have a buyer who is looking for a battle of attrition to get the best deal. Being told that your company has been selected for final negotiations does not put you a strong position. In fact you may concede too much just to close the deal. If your buyer is particularly slippery, it may just be a ruse, as the threat to go back to one or more of the competitors may jerk you into agreeing more than is sensible.

It is important to stress to your sales team who may be in this position that the selling is not over until that clean order is received. This can be a very stressful time for most sales people. You need to be supportive while justifying certain negotiation boundaries you have set. While you could be accused of not appreciating the situation, you may, in fact, have a better and more balanced view. It comes down to whether you trust the sales team and whether they trust you.

The best relationship with a customer is one of partnership. Here, last minute battles with a buyer are rare as both sides value give and take for mutual benefit. They are the normal practice for the most senior sales people. Unfortunately, life is not always like that. There is value in specific training in negotiation techniques. Buyers go on courses to learn hand-to-hand combat with sales people. You should do the same with your staff. There is a limited number of common buyer tactics and your staff should know how to recognise them and devise counter-strategies.

Most sales people are measured by the revenue or margin contribution they gain for the company. While this can be measured by orders received, it is better to measure when the invoice has been issued. It means that, while the actual selling cycle is complete, a responsibility for the customer lasts until delivery and acceptance. If the invoice is issued only when you have discharged your obligations, any open or poorly defined conditions agreed by your sales person may delay the dispatch of the invoice. Hence, the sale is not recognised to that sales person. It may be harsh but the job of a good sales person is to get good, clean, predictable business. You may want to modify this if the nature of your business makes it an unacceptable disincentive. In general though, the sales team need to work within the constraints of good business practice.

As a trusted manager and excellent communicator of business risk and practice, you have explained all the above to the team. They will now never give up until a quality order is received. As for your sales person who has beaten the competition but not got the order, he came to see you merely to discuss a point of strategy. This agreed, he departs to appear some time later, red in tooth and claw, and clutching a sheet of paper and smiling broadly.

Training

It has been mentioned several times in this book that selling is a complex job requiring high intellectual capital. It was also pointed out at the beginning that there are few, if any, degree level courses that include selling as distinct from marketing. With little academic input to the profession, it has been left to a variety of training companies to provide theory and structure to the job. There have been well known sales schools as part of some multi-nationals. Rank Zerox gave excellent training to photocopier sales people. The IBM sales school not only gave a though grounding to its own staff but also spawned off several other training organisations.

For most organisations without an internal training department, there is no choice but to use training companies. Some of these companies develop their own material but there are several respected franchised courses which have become almost expected in certain industries. Which is the right one for you is down to much time spent studying the brochures, cost and length of the course.

Before spending huge amounts of money on training, there is something you need to know and never forget. If you are having trouble getting a sales person to perform, then sending them on a training course will not be a scrap of use. If you hired a dog when you wanted a lion then no amount of role-plays and checklists will do the transformation. Training is most useful when you have employed the raw talent and now need to give direction, focus and planning. Anyone who has been on a training course has met the participants who are there because their manager hopes for a miracle.

What then should training do for your team? I suggest there are two types of training that are useful; firstly those which impart skills, secondly, information that improves their quality of approach.

Examples of the first could be:

- negotiation with buyers
- account management
- the selling cycle
- territory management.

The second group could be:

- legal
- finance
- industry or market overviews.

The topics above recognise that in getting good clean orders, there are barriers, challenges and opportunities based on a wide knowledge of the whole business environment. A sound understanding of company finance can allow convincing value propositions to be put in front of the customer. Legal knowledge will prevent you from subsequently appearing in the dock. As sales staff develop their careers, these wider skills become more crucial. If you want your top sales people to meet the top people in their accounts, make sure they are well equipped. Another point here; do you and your sales team read the business sections of quality newspapers regularly? Do you subscribe to relevant trade journals? Training and education goes on all the time.

10

Commissions and Bonuses

Why are sales people paid commission and bonuses? Other employees are frequently paid an annual bonus but it rarely amounts to very much. It is certainly not embedded in expectations in the same way as in the sales function. The plain answer is that there is no reason to pay sales people in a different way from the rest of the organisation. So, if you manage everyone else the same as your sales team and have the same expectations, you target and measure them relentlessly and make their successes and failures public, then pay them all the same way. That may not go down too well. Also, it does go a bit deeper than simply how you manage. It has a lot to do with the culture of your company. If everyone strives to achieve, is motivated and proud of what they do, then the way you compensate the sales people should be similar to the rest of the staff. How much they are paid will depend more on market conditions to get the quality you need. A point about greed and sales staff. Lots of people are greedy. Not many have the skills to be capable sales people. Do not confuse a desire to earn lots of money with the capability and skills to do so.

So, why pay the sales team commission or bonuses, as an alternative is to pay only a good salary. There are three reasons why you may consider it.

1. It is common and expected in your industry

You may want to be able to break free of the culture of your industry but the risk is that the better sales people see it as a limitation.

2. You want the sales people to move out of their comfort zone

If you want people to move out of their comfort zone or stretch further than they are used to, then money is one encouragement. A key point about selling, at least with high performance selling, is that nothing happens until the sales person does something. That something is often difficult.

3. You think your sales team will work harder

This is the normal reason for paying commission. With most of the team out of sight and therefore out of direct supervision, the carrot of money becomes more relevant than the stick of control. A sentiment of 'if they don't sell, they don't eat' underpins much of the culture of commission.

It is easy to get distracted by the issue of commission and see it as crucial to the success of the sales team and therefore to the success of the company. A bit of history is worth telling to put these incentives in context. In the 1980s, there were three significant and interesting computer companies (yes, I know there were more than three) Digital Equipment Company, also known as DEC, IBM and Sun Microsystems. DEC started in the late 1950s and by the beginning of the 1980s, had become the world's second largest computer company after IBM. The products and the company were well respected with the founder, Ken Olsen, eventually making the front page of *Time Magazine* as entrepreneur of the year. During the 1980s, it was phenomenally successful. It was the only major computer company that did not pay commission to the sales force. It paid good but not excessive salaries.

IBM was, and still is, the world's largest computer company. It also had a good 1980s when it consolidated a grip on the computer market only exceeded later by Microsoft. It paid moderate commissions on top of reasonable base salaries.

Sun Microsystems started in 1983 and grew rapidly by selling UNIX based workstations. They took the market by storm and out-paced and out-thought the attempts by DEC and IBM to launch their own workstation products and recapture the market. Later a successful server range was launched. Sun paid a high level of commission with numerous bonuses. A Sun sales person could earn perhaps double that of the equivalent DEC or IBM person.

Come the 1990s and the world began to change. DEC allowed its technology to lag and its proprietary systems lost favour against more open standards. It had no stranglehold on mainframe computers, unlike IBM, so it fell into losses. As a desperate measure to keep staff, it introduced bonuses for the sales teams but to no avail. It was taken over by Compaq in 1997.

IBM also hit problems in the mid-nineties. Wrong-footed by Microsoft and facing a declining mainframe business, IBM shed thousands of staff and lost its dominance of the computer market. Hiring the head of a biscuit manufacturer, Lou Gerstner from Nabisco, as CEO was an astonishing move but did the trick. Today a reformed IBM is still strong but not controlling the markets as it did in previous decades.

Sun Microsystems, the upstart workstation company, grew at an astonishing pace while DEC and IBM stuttered. It had moved into large servers, launched the computer nerds favourite language, Java, and became totally associated with the internet boom. At the end of the nineties, it looked impregnable. Then the dot.com boom bombed and so did Sun. The shares collapsed from $64 and finally bottomed at less then $3. Heavy losses and redundancies took the heat out of Sun.

What is the lesson of the above? All three companies had excellent sales teams; well motivated, proud of their employer, capable and well trained. The fact that the compensation of the sales function was very different in each case played no part in the success of the eighties or the stress of the nineties. The company fortunes were governed by the quality of top-level strategic leadership, their products and the state of the market. How these companies retained excellent sales teams while compensating in very different ways is worth a book in itself. The point is that there is no iron rule about commissions or bonuses in the selling function and the success of your company.

Assuming that you do want your sales force to have financial incentives, then take time for a look at how to do it. As before, it all starts with your business plan and what you want to achieve. Incentives must be structured to deliver objectives that drive your business in a certain direction. The downside is that other desirable motives may be dumped or ignored if they distract from money-making endeavours. The result is that a single bonus or commission goal is rarely adequate in most sales situations, let alone the more complex.

Bonuses are the most straightforward incentive. A bonus payment means a specific sum is paid once a specific objective is agreed. The need to be accurate to the point of being pedantic in setting objectives has been spelt out in the chapter on Getting Organised. The advantage of bonus payments is that they can be precise in motivating people to achieve targets that are clearly in the business plan. They are not open-ended so there are limits on any liabilities that can occur with commissions. There can be a range of bonus targets to direct sales behaviour across a broad range of objectives. Bonuses can be most effective when you have specific targets where gross over achievement or no action at all would be detrimental to the business. The downside for the sales people is that bonuses are binary; miss the target slightly and you miss the bonus completely.

Commission has always been the favourite incentive for sales forces. Work harder and you get more money. If a sales person is not successful, then at least their salary bill is lower. In manufacturing, getting paid for what you make – piecework – has fallen completely out of favour, while, curiously, in sales the equivalent is still going strong. Perhaps this is a reflection of the lack of academic rigour in sales work and a perceived element of smoke and mirrors. With sales people out of the office so much, management control falls back to metering the money. Having said that, commission does focus the mind. As it is so powerful, it has to be structured carefully to avoid the inevitable distortions it encourages.

The first matter to decide is the proportion of compensation that is fixed, that is the base salary, and the amount that is variable, the commission. Normally, the commission is based on achieving the set sales target; this commission plus the base salary adds up to the On Target Earnings (OTE). It is known, though rare, to have a commission-only sales team. There is hardly any need to have sales people as employees with this arrangement. You might as well have independent agents. The range in proportion of base salary to commission commonly varies from about 40% base and 60% commission to 90% base and 10% commission.

Generally speaking, the shorter the sales cycle and more regular the orders, the lower the base salary in proportion to OTE. A fully competent sales person bringing in regular business will be close to OTE each month. At the other extreme, long complex sales would leave the sales person on base salary for much of the time. This would be de-motivating; hence a higher base. Having stated this, there are no rules. It comes down to how you want to run and motivate the team. Let us be quite frank about commission payments. You can use commission to be the cream on top of success. Alternatively you can use it so that poor performers leave as they can't make any money and greed will motivate the best. This is lazy management and makes nonsense of careful selection of staff, career paths and rewards for long-term commitment. So is there any justification for a highly commissioned environment? Perhaps, if the risk is high, and success is based on stretching way beyond the comfort zone and a high degree of creative or lateral thinking. Take care though when writing the sales agreement in these cases. You want clean business, happy customers and profit. You don't want to be sweeping up after your selling Exocet.

There is a bit more to commissions. They can be fine-tuned to encourage or discourage certain behaviours. The first, and most common, tinkering with the system is whether the commission is capped. There are three reasons for capping commission. One is that you want to limit your financial liabilities. An unexpected large commission payment could give problems though commission in theory pays for itself. You may want to discourage too much business if it gives production difficulties. If the targets are accurately matched to factory capacity, then over-selling by a significant amount may not be worth the effort. Lastly, you may have concerns over team dynamics. Not all over-achievement in selling is due to hard work. Chance and opportunity play a part. Large payments that do not correspond to large efforts can have a corrosive effect on a team. Before introducing a cap, just consider why you have a commission structure in the first place. If it is there as a strong incentive and a significant proportion of earnings are commission, then a cap defeats the whole point. Commission is a shared risk and incentive.

The second tuning is changing the commission rate at various points. Instead of a linear rate between the base and OTE points, the rate of commission can be varied to limit payments close to base and accelerate them close to OTE. This is to stop sales people cruising because they have earned enough money. After OTE, the rate of commission can be increased to encourage over-achievement. After, say, 120%, the commission could be doubled. Alternatively, it can be decreased to discourage too much business.

The third tuning is to change commissions on an ad hoc basis to deal with specific issues, such as increasing commission for the last week in a quarter or financial year to get any last minute business in. Is a product slow moving? Give more commission to move it.

Just remember that, as you tinker with commission, it sets up behaviours that you may not want. Capping can let sales people lose focus once the maximum has been sold. They can also sandbag an order until a new quarter or year starts. While you may want this to keep the order flow consistent, you can lose the customer as well as the order. If you want to encourage over-achievement, also ensure quality of customer care. Paying a large lump of commission for an order that will later be thrown back at you is not good business. Remember that once you try to harness avarice to drive your business, then management theory gives way to raw emotion.

Once the bonuses and commissions are out of the way the other aspects of compensation are straightforward. Private health, share schemes, pensions and so on are the same as for the rest of the company. That just leaves the company car. After commission and target setting whinges, the company car is next in line to wind you up. The company car is a statement about lifestyle, status, self-esteem and, lastly, the method to visit customers. Most repmobile cars are now capable of transporting a sales person safely and comfortably between appointments. Your team will spend a fair amount of time behind the wheel, so don't be mean with air conditioning and a CD player. If you feel that the team should be shod with the classier examples of German engineering, then go ahead. Just remember, few sales people are satisfied with their car. There is always one better and the neighbour has it. Draw a line on what you provide but give a cash option. The car obsessed can then bankrupt themselves and not you.

11

Alternatives

You've had enough of running a sales force. They are too expensive, demanding, out of control and not earning their keep. On the other hand, you may not have a sales force yet and don't want to get one. Your expertise could be in design or production. Perhaps your location means that the sales team would always be remote from the office. However, whether you like or loath sales, you need to get more business or you go out of business. Is there any other way to do it?

There are other ways that may replace your sales function or, at least, contain the costs while allowing sales to grow. It is wise to remember that whatever you do there is a cost attached to it; there is no zero cost of sale. Here are some alternatives to an on-the-road field sales force.

- Use agents, resellers, distributors or other third party selling organisation.
- Only use an internal sales function.
- Use direct mail or advertising.
- Use the internet.

There may be others but the above are worth a look. It is likely that no one sales channel above will be adequate but a combination of two or three will be needed to reinforce each other. Let us look in detail at these alternatives.

- **Use agents, resellers, distributors or other third party selling organisation**

There are some industries, products or services that demand the use of a sales force. If this is the case with you, then you need some sort of organisation that wants to do sales. Sales and marketing companies can do more than just take on your selling. They can bring you into markets that you have no experience of or means of accessing. Even if you want to keep and develop your sales force, third party selling can rapidly increase business.

Agents are commonly individuals or partnerships that represent your company but do not buy directly from you and then sell on. Their job is to find customers and persuade them of the merits of your product. You may have to issue quotations or proposals as a result of their activities. If successful, the order is placed directly on your company. Agents are usually paid a commission based on the net value of the order. If the agents are individuals, they often ask for a retainer to cover expenses, particularly when starting with your product. When working out the commission and retainer, remember that the agent is replacing the costs of the field sales person but all the other support activities need to be in place. Your company will still have a direct relationship with the end user and be bound by your terms and conditions of sale.

The main benefit of agents is often thought to be that if they do not sell, they do not get paid. While this is true, it is not a wise basis for a selling strategy. Agents in the UK and export can have expertise in markets where you have no experience. They can develop business for you at low cost and low risk assuming your product is suitable. They can also sell for you in markets or territories which do not justify a full-time sales person. Therefore do not think of agents as simply a replacement for a direct sales force, but they can compliment very effectively.

What are the disadvantages? As the agent is not an employee, you have no direct control. Furthermore, the agent is unlikely to only represent your products. It is probable that the agent was chosen due to a successful track record of selling something else into your chosen market. You will have to fight for diary time and ensure that representing your product is worthwhile for the agent. Agents can be similar to employed sales people in that they require the same level of support. The demands for brochures, quotations, technical data and everything yesterday will not change.

Resellers are the next step up. They will buy from you and sell on to their customers. Your customer is the reseller and you have no contract with the end user. The advantages are similar to agents but resellers can add more value and relieve you of some of the administration. They should issue quotations, provide support, sometimes service and do some marketing. The best thing about resellers is that they should have their own sales team and sales management. It is normal to have several resellers, each concentrating on a territory or market and owning the quality of relationship with the customer. Their other products can be complimentary to yours or even integrate with your products to give a more compelling reason to buy. They buy from you at a discount and use this margin to fund their business. Retainers are unusual but some help towards marketing costs are normal.

Unlike agents, resellers can reduce your costs of sale substantially due to moving to them most of the selling administration. As you are not dealing with a large number of end users but a smaller number of resellers you can ship in bulk to fewer destinations. Like agents, you have access to more markets and many more sales people then you could afford. They can handle first line customer support and service. Many industries make good use of resellers to reinforce a core direct sales force. The most obvious example is car dealers but the computer and software industry has used resellers to reduce the costs of a complex sale.

Is it all benefits and no problems? Not quite. Good resellers do not come cheap so expect steep discounts to attract and keep the best. Just as with agents you rely on the competence of staff you do not employ and who may have other routes to earning money. It is common with resellers that they have competitive products though they may split the sales teams to reduce conflict. No direct contact with the end users is a double-edged sword. It can be satisfactory when all is well. When things go pear shaped, the reseller can get slippery leaving you to sort out the mess. If you do not have access to or even know who the end users are, how do you promote your products if you suspect the reseller is not doing a good job?

Distributors are a variant of resellers. They will have a number of resellers, shops, manufacturers of substantial end users as customers. It is a matter of judgement whether the product or market can support extending the supply line with more parties taking a margin. Here, you are even further from the end user with its advantages and disadvantages.

All the above are viable routes to market that aim to off-load much of the selling effort from you while ensuring that the business still flows in. The catch is that to make these channels successful, you have to work at it. It is just not possible to set up agents, resellers and distributors and then turn your attention to something else. You have to constantly nurture these relationships to achieve the best results. In the real world you will be constantly recruiting new agents to replace the non-performers or to close gaps in the market. It is similar with resellers but this is a more business-to-business relationship and some resellers can be very demanding customers. As soon as you export and choose to start with some third party representation, you have all the above plus local culture.

As you expand, you end up recruiting a sales person again to handle what are really customers by a different name. This type of sales person, commonly called Channel Marketing Manager or similar, is there to recruit and maintain good relationships with businesses that will be closer to you than an end user. You will have to carefully recruit and inspire a whole external organisation so, far from disengaging from selling, you can find yourself pretty well joined at the hip to the reseller. If it goes well you can have access to a professional sales force who can ramp up business far faster than you could ever have managed on your own.

A final point about using any of these channels. Get a lawyer. Two main reasons for this. While any relationship starts with hope, sweetness and light, when it goes bad, it is best to know exactly where you stand. Unless you are particularly neurotic or have unique requirements, there are standard agreements you can use. The second is to do with European Community law on competition. Falling foul of this can be ruinously expensive. Setting up exclusive territories, using discount structures to favour one reseller over another and so on could bring you to the attention of Brussels and heaps of bother. If you feel your product or service does need specialist attention and so you want to be choosy over how it is sold and by whom, then get advice. There are legal ways and means if you want to restrict who represents you, so there is no reason to use illegal means.

• Only use an internal sales function

The advantage of the internal sales function is that they are in the office and part of the normal office management and disciplines. What they do can be tightly monitored and the results analysed. Their call rate is much higher than the road warriors and they are so much cheaper to run. A variant of the internal sales team is the call centre. I suggest the difference is that in the call centre the sales effort can be reduced to a specific script with a limited sales proposition. In this case, the whole selling effort could be given over to specialist call centres.

Of course, this all depends on what you are selling. While there are some products or services that will always require a call from a sales person in person, there are others that now rarely need a face-to-face discussion. This is a constantly moving trend and it is accelerated by the need to take cost out of the supply of any product or service. There is a pressure to move design, manufacture and supply to the cheapest route given minimum levels of quality and buyer acceptability.

If you do not have an internal selling function, start one. Do not try asking the sales administrators or others who may have just answered the phone on behalf of the sales team to do a bit of selling instead of passing the call on. Selling is selling which means trained, focused specialists who have a specific, defined role. You may get conflict and boundary disputes with the road team or resellers, particularly if there is a commission scheme. Monitor and keep close to the action while it beds in. Success is based on whether you have moved lower value orders, or customers to the internal team and so reduced the costs of sale. This does not mean reduce quality of customer care. The contact for the customer is always in the office, just a phone call away. If there are issues with quality or response, you can deal with it quickly.

Having a good internal sales function may not eliminate the road warriors but you can aim them at high-value opportunities. You should be looking always at pulling more business onto the internal team to reduce costs. There will be some instances where the flexible selling skills of the internal team are overkill. If you want to do a specific campaign such as selling service contracts or a new accessory and the proposition can be reduced to a simple script, then consider a call centre. Again, the advantage is a lower cost of call and a higher call rate. Remember to keep it simple though.

• Direct mail or advertising

With the internal sales function, you have removed the face-to-face aspect of selling but retained flexibility and relationship. If some or all of your selling could sacrifice that as well, then look at marketing channels. Marketing is outside the scope of this book but there are many other books and experts. You may have to rethink your whole business to make this channel effective but it has been successfully tried.

• The internet

In the eighteenth century, there was the South Sea Bubble, the nineteenth century gave us the railway mania and the twentieth the internet. The money may have evaporated but we still have the stock exchange, railways and the internet. While it may have got over-blown, the internet is still very important. Your company should have a website; it should be up to date and should be a core part of your company's promotion and identity. Can you move from internet presence towards e-business? Specifically, the question here is, can it replace your field sales team?

A key advantage of web technology is that it is dynamic. You can incorporate the means for the customer to use options, tools, information, links and possible costs. Hence the customer can build a possible solution in a low-pressure environment. This activity takes away from the sales person the mechanical or feeding information aspects of the job. What then is left to be done? Really, only the aspects of selling that are the most difficult and mark out the best performing sales people from the rest – relationship building, persuasion, positioning against the competition, advice of the kind that approaches wisdom. And pressing for the order. How much do you need these skills? Or the tougher question, do you actually have them anyway?

Before getting carried away with the internet, it should be remembered that this channel rarely stands by itself. Your website will not drop onto a prospect's desk with the words, 'use me' uttered in a beguiling manner. You have to persuade people to make the effort to access your site. That assumes your target contact has good access to the internet and will make the significant step to making it the primary contact with your company. Internet trading is usually backed up with direct mail and a telephone help desk or call centre. The cost of marketing was significant in the bombing of the early web pioneers. There is no excuse now for e-business naivety.

What has characterised the growth of other selling channels from just having a sales force or only direct mail is the complex integration of the old and the new. Added to this is the way products can start complex and need specialist direct selling but by branding and familiarity become commodity, sold by price and features. The pressure to do this comes from the need to reduce costs while maintaining an adequate level of customer care. Most successful businesses now operate a mixture of selling channels to reflect their market, give value for money and maximise their reach. Computer-based systems for customer relationship managements, call centre management and e-business can allow a customer to move from an internet-based browser, to a telephone helpline and finally to a visit from a sales person.

In ditching the sales force, you have to consider whether your product or market can do some of the selling itself. Moving to low cost channels can result in low cost products. Never underestimate the power of price. Having said that, for some products or services, the old sales maxim applies; being there is half the battle.

Index